DROPPING THE BOMB

edited by

John Gladwin

HODDER AND STOUGHTON
LONDON   SYDNEY   AUCKLAND   TORONTO

British Library cataloguing in Publication data

Gladwin, John
  Dropping the bomb.
  1. Atomic weapons—Religious aspects—
Christianity   2. Atomic weapons—Great Britain
I. Title
261.8'73   BT736.2

ISBN 0 340 37247 8

*Printed in Great Britain for Hodder and Stoughton Limited, Mill Road, Dunton
Green, Sevenoaks, Kent by Richard Clay (The Chaucer Press) Limited, Bungay,
Suffolk. Photoset by Rowland Phototypesetting Limited, Bury St Edmunds,
Suffolk. Hodder and Stoughton Editorial Office: 47 Bedford Square, London
WC1B 3DP.*

CONTENTS

PREFACE

How can we help to make and to maintain peace in a world under the threat of the nuclear bomb? Such is one of the most urgent and serious questions facing all of us today. None of us can escape wrestling with it. The Christian Church, if it is to be true in its witness to the Prince of Peace, must share in the world's struggle to find an answer to it.

This is exactly what the Churches have been seeking to do. Building on a long tradition of responding to the moral demands of questions of war and violence, the Church has been wrestling with the challenge of the nuclear bomb. This book is designed to be an aid to church members who want to begin to understand some of the ramifications of this issue. The large debates of Church assemblies and specialist groups need the response and contribution of the whole Christian community. This book introduces concerned lay people to the central issues and to the debate going on in the conscience of the Church.

We begin with the reflections of David Edwards, Provost of Southwark, on the great debate held in the General Synod of the Church of England on February 10th, 1983, in response to the report, *The Church and the Bomb*, produced by a Board for Social Responsibility Working Party chaired by the Bishop of Salisbury. On this historic day the nation listened in to the Church wrestling with the challenge of peace in the age of the bomb. The debate goes on.

Any serious discussion of the problems requires a basic grasp of weapons development and deployment. Frank Barnaby, former Director of SIPRI and at present working for Just Defence, sets out the chilling information about the present situation and raises some uncomfortable questions as a result. This leads into thinking about strategies. The Church of England's General Synod came down in favour of a 'no first-use' strategy, which it believes makes sense of the Christian moral demand. General Sir Hugh Beach, Warden of St George's House, Windsor since 1981, Vice Lord Lieutenant of Greater London since 1981 and Chief Royal Engineer since 1982, sets out what a no first-use strategy might mean if we adopted it.

At the heart of the ethical debate lies the question of deterrence. Can deterrence be squared with responsible Christian theology and ethics? Dr Alan Kreider, Director of the London Mennonite Centre, and for many years a student of the theological issues, believes that it is not possible for Christians who are either pacifists or believers in the Just War theory to support policies of deterrence. The Revd Richard Harries, Dean of King's College, London, and, like Dr Kreider, a major contributor to the debate, believes that it is possible, in principle, for Christians to support the notion of deterrence. In working on these contributions readers will be able to test out and develop their own Christian ethical approach.

What have the traditional themes of Christian theology to contribute to the forming of our minds? The Bishop of Kensington, the Rt Revd Mark Santer, sets out the Christian meaning of peace and its implications. Canon Douglas Rhymes, a member of the General Synod and of the Board for Social Responsibility, and until recently Vicar of Woldingham, considers the meaning of the wisdom tradition in Christian thought for the issues. Lord Blanch, formerly Archbishop of York, who made a notable contribution to the February General Synod debate, helps us to think through the meaning of Christian faith about the future. He encourages us to live by faith in God's good purposes for the future.

Where is this debate going? The Bishop of Salisbury, who chaired the Working Party which produced *The Church and the Bomb*, reflects on what the Church should be about in carrying on its stated commitment to these matters. John Selwyn Gummer, MP, member of the General Synod, Chairman of the Conservative Party and Minister of State at the Department of Employment, sets out what he believes is the way forward to peace in the present international situation.

Each contributor seeks to persuade the reader of an argument. That the contributions when taken together represent contrasting as well as complementary approaches is indicative of the fact that a serious debate is continuing in the Churches. We hope that the questions set out at the end of each chapter help the reader to respond to what has been offered. They may be of value to those who wish to use the book as a basis for group discussion of the issues.

I am grateful to all the contributors for responding so enthusiastically, as well as with great skill, to my request to write for this symposium. I am grateful to the Board for Social Responsibility for all its work on the subject of defence and peace and for agreeing to my taking on this task. The Board is not, however, responsible for any of the views expressed in this book. They remain the personal contributions of the authors. Finally, I am grateful to Brenda Stanley, my secretary, who has in her unfailingly patient and skilful way, typed the manuscript through a number of drafts and carried out most of the administrative work associated with preparing this text.

JOHN GLADWIN

Section I

THE CHURCH AND THE BOMB

1 THE GREAT DEBATE
The Very Revd David L. Edwards

On February 10th, 1983, the great debate about the morality of nuclear weapons had a new focus. The scene was very different from Congress or Parliament, the corridors of military power, the streets filled with banner-carrying demonstrators, or the clinically safe atmosphere of the control rooms from which the missiles may one day be fired to end our civilisation. This time many eyes were on Church House, Westminster. In the yard outside, around the great lawn in the shadow of Westminster Abbey, there were queues of people impatient to listen to the churchmen's debate. Inside the building reporters from papers neither religious nor English looked puzzled by this assignment, and technicians were busy, for this debate was going to be televised and broadcast live. The members of the General Synod of the Church of England, scarcely believing that they were to be the centre of such attention, had to arrive early if they were to secure seats in the circular debating hall, which was heated as well as lit by the TV lamps. Those who could not be accommodated downstairs had to sit in the gallery, where they (but not the public alongside them) were allowed to applaud. Many felt the pleasant tingle of drama. Do not demonstrators have some fun on a day out? Do not servicemen enjoy a sense of duty done? The human race persists in being human when the alternative is total terror and despair.

In July 1979 the Synod, grateful for 'the Church's role in preserving and promoting peace', had asked its Board for Social Responsibility to explore how 'the theological debate relating to discipleship in this field might be more effectively and purposefully conducted throughout the Church of England in the light of the witness and insights of the whole ecumenical movement'. The very language of this resolution betrayed its origins, which might brutally be called parsonical. The Board had set up a working party which had begun to meet a year after the passing of the resolution. It was asked 'to study the implications for Christian discipleship of the acceptance by the major military powers of a role for thermonuclear weapons in their strategy' and 'to consider the bearing of this on the adequacy of past Christian teaching and ethical analysis regarding the conduct of war'. Obviously such an exercise could be controversial, for 'the whole ecumenical movement', or at least bodies such as the World and British Councils of Churches, had often denounced nuclear weapons and this 'witness' was in conflict with the policies of successive British governments and the preferences of the majority of the British electorate. It may have been significant that the reference to the 'witness and insights of the whole ecumenical movement' was not repeated in the working party's more precise terms of reference. What the working party was asked to do now sounded like an educational or academic exercise, rather than a challenge to the facts of British political and military life.

The seven men appointed were not well-known as bold radicals. The only exception was Paul Oestreicher, a member of the General Synod and a Secretary of the British Council of Churches, often attacked or teased in the *Daily Telegraph* and elsewhere as a left-wing pacifist. The others were (and are) all gentle, donnish moderates. Dr John Elford teaches social and pastoral theology in the University of Manchester, and Dr Barrie Paskins, a philosopher, lectures in war studies at King's College, London. The group's secretary, Giles Ecclestone, was then the Secretary to the Board for Social Responsibility; a former Clerk in the House of Commons, he was about to become a student for the Anglican priesthood. The original reference to the insights of non-Anglicans in the ecumenical movement helped to explain the presence of a

Quaker (Sydney Bailey, a much respected scholar in international affairs and Chairman of the Council on Christian Approaches to Defence and Disarmament), and a Roman Catholic priest (Brendan Soane, a lecturer in moral theology). The chairman was John Austin Baker, for many years an Oxford theologian, and then a Canon of Westminster with special responsibility for the historic St Margaret's Church and the chaplaincy in the House of Commons – a scholarly pastor who was about to be appointed, on Mrs Thatcher's recommendation, to be bishop of the rural and mainly conservative diocese of Salisbury. It was a small group, but one well qualified to assess Christian theology and discipleship. The absence of politicians, defence chiefs and diplomats, active or retired, spoke eloquently about the expected character of its work; but it was known that some of its members, including its Chairman, started out from a position opposed to unilateral disarmament by Britain.

Why then, on that February day in Westminster, did excitement surround the presentation of *The Church and the Bomb*,[1] a report which had already become a bestseller? And why were some commentators taking it as evidence that the Church of England had resigned from the Establishment – or had been kicked out of it? When, back in August, there had been a leak about the report's contents, Julian Amery, MP, had warned, 'There is clearly an element in the Church which is heading for confrontation with the State.' A Conservative colleague, Michael Bretherton, had labelled the report 'the latest example of the trendies attempting to take over the Church'. 'There could be nothing more immoral,' thundered Winston Churchill, MP. 'Maggie is furious', headlined the *Sun*; 'Runcie joins in new row' claimed the *Daily Mail* (the Archbishop had pointed out that the report was not an official document of the Church). But, of course, those who liked the thought of the Church confronting the State, or who were themselves 'trendies' protesting that nothing could be more immoral than the use of nuclear weapons, or who belonged more quietly to the 'peace movement', had greeted with applause the news that a working party appointed by the Established Church had agreed on this kind of report. In the world of religious publishing there had been no similar phenomenon since the stormy launching twenty years earlier of Bishop John Robinson's *Honest to God*,[2] which had questioned the popular image of God as a person 'out there'. That paperback had popularised philosophical theology. Now *The Church and the Bomb* had made sure that for the British public moral theology was no longer 'out there'.

A comparison between this report and *Honest to God* is illuminating. Neither book achieved its immense impact by being simple. The language in each was often technical, and the bomb book had at its end a glossary of the jargon of its nightmarish science seven pages long. The conclusions reached often seemed confused. Both books reached a wide public precisely because both challenged their readers to join in the debate – and because both had the courage needed to emerge out of an academic or ecclesiastical ghetto in order to tackle basic human questions. Is God real and if so how is he (or she, or it) best pictured? Is God in control of life on this planet, or is our nuclear doom inescapable and near? If Doomsday is optional, how best can it be avoided? When writing *Honest to God* and *The Church and the Bomb*, men who were clever, good and privileged were willing to be denounced as fools or knaves in order to think aloud about such questions; and in the event they paid a price. But the attention given demonstrated that Britain is not a nation totally indifferent to problems of religion and morality.

The bishop who wrote *Honest to God* would have aroused less anger had he not confessed that problems about how to think about God, and how to pray, troubled him personally. The authors of *The Church and the Bomb* would have stirred up less fury – and less interest – had they stopped before making recommendations about British policy. 'On these general approaches to the problem one might hope for a consensus', they claimed – after advocating serious disarmament negotiations, a more concerned and informed national awareness of defence policies, collaboration between all

nations in the tasks of peace, and a call to the Churches to
'pray, preach and practise peace'.

Confined to such generalities, their report might have had
much resemblance to *The Challenge of Peace: God's Promise
and Our Response*, the Pastoral Letter approved on May 8th,
1983, by the Roman Catholic Bishops of the United States.
That document was an excellent summary of the teaching on
war and peace in the Catholic Church since the Sermon on the
Mount, and its own message was summed up in a quotation
from Pope John Paul II (to the United Nations on June 11th,
1982). 'In current conditions "deterrence" based on balance,
certainly not as an end in itself but as a step on the way
towards a progressive disarmament, may still be judged
morally acceptable. Nonetheless, in order to ensure peace, it
is indispensable not to be satisfied with this minimum which
is always susceptible to the real danger of explosion.'

To be sure, these bishops had incurred the wrath of many
of their fellow Americans by saying that this teaching implied
that 'no *use* of nuclear weapons which would violate the
principles of discrimination or proportionality may be *intended* in a strategy of deterrence' (the italics are theirs). They
had added that 'we do not perceive any situation in which the
deliberate initiation of nuclear war, on however restricted a
scale, can be morally justified. Non-nuclear attacks by
another state must be resisted by other than nuclear means.'

But their stress was on principles, not on more detailed and
therefore controversial policies. They did not condemn the
possession of indiscriminate weapons or their use if not
intended 'for the purpose of destroying population centres or
other predominantly civilian targets' – and these qualifications might in time of war justify the destruction of Moscow
for the sake of its military targets.

The British group was now much less cautious, producing
a report which by its courage attracted more hostility than
had been bestowed on a long line of documents to which the
British Churches had previously given birth – a line stretch-
ing back to *The Era of Atomic Power* in 1946. For they
recommended that whether or not the USSR responded, the

UK should renounce its independent nuclear deterrent, abandon its smaller nuclear weapons whether of British or American manufacture, end all US air- and submarine-base facilities which brought nuclear weapons on to our soil, and refuse to house the Cruise missiles due to arrive from the USA. It was no small programme.

They still seemed confused because they wished Britain to remain within NATO and therefore under the American nuclear umbrella – and because even the British withdrawal from the nuclear evil was to be phased in negotiation with allies. 'Total abandonment of nuclear weapons by one of the alliances in the international line-up could undoubtedly have serious destabilising effects' they recognised – but 'as a policy option . . . it lies in the realms of fantasy as things are at present'. They therefore laid themselves open to the charge of wanting to eat the cake of moral purity while prudently keeping in the cupboard the cake of political prudence with American nuclear missiles as its chief decoration.

But they had said enough to start a major row. For their report recommended that on these key questions of defence the Church of England should line itself up with the left wing of the Labour Party – and should do this in a year which was to bring about a Conservative electoral triumph. The challenge was to the Church to stop sitting on the fence – in a year when not even the need to ally against Labour and the Tories could make the Liberals and the Social Democrats agree on a clear policy about nuclear weapons. The hope was of a great step forward in disarmament – in a year which was to see the continued expansion of Soviet military might, Congressional approval for President Reagan's MX missiles, and the advent of the Cruise and Pershing missiles to Europe. No wonder that the *Daily Mail* reckoned that 'the Church is becoming too big politically for its gaiters'!

On January 29th almost a whole page of *The Times* was devoted to an article by Paul Johnson, formerly editor of the *New Statesman* but now a budding Conservative intellectual. After a summary of the complicated history of Christian attitudes to war, he concluded, 'It is hard to see how it can be lawful to use thermonuclear weapons except against isolated military targets, and the use of tactical and battlefield nuclear weapons must clearly be very restricted.' But that conclusion was followed by others. 'Precisely because war is so infinitely corrupting, and because the means at the disposal of those so corrupted are of such colossal magnitude, the need to prevent war becomes absolutely paramount.' Therefore 'the positive moral significance of deterrence is overwhelming' and it is of the greatest importance that the acceptance of *The Church and the Bomb* could well begin the erosion of the NATO concept of collective security and 'restraints on America's own deterrent which would destroy its credibility', thus tempting 'forward moves' by the USSR. 'It is difficult to conceive of circumstances more likely to risk a major war, in which thermonuclear weapons would certainly be used, and a war which, after appalling destruction, the Soviets would win.' The alternative would be a peace amounting to 'the global imposition of state communism', the triumph of a system which has a 'structural propensity to evil'. In these circumstances 'it could plausibly be asserted that pacificism, and especially militant and proselytizing pacifism, is itself a great moral evil'. Indeed, 'it is obligatory for Christians to subscribe to deterrence'. But for a Christian in the nuclear age, deterrence involves the development of modernised, more accurate, missiles with military targets, and the improvement of civil defence. Such arguments also ran through speeches by political advocates of the Conservative Government's policies, although without Paul Johnson's references to church history and also without his emphasis on the possibility of restricting nuclear weapons to military targets. Whether or not the courtesies of debate were preserved, the impression was conveyed that the churchmen who had urged 'one-sided' nuclear disarmament for Britain had exposed themselves as bungling amateurs, men carrying lighted church candles into places which stored material far more explosive than gunpowder.

However, the group that made unanimous recommendations in *The Church and the Bomb* did so by a carefully considered route. Ronald Butt in *The Times* alleged that the working party was 'weighted in one direction' by the active pacifists with 'strong personalities' and that its report was 'without guiding moral or theological principles'. But Sydney Bailey, the Quaker scholar, could reply by denying that theirs was a pacifist report – and by stressing that although 'the working party was deliberately set up so as to have a balanced composition', yet 'opinions changed while we were at work'. These opinions included moral and political judgments. Looking back over the controversy, Bishop Baker later wrote that 'in the area of ethics the report raised at least five basic questions that will not go away: 1. Are there some weapons so dreadful that it could never be right to use them? 2. Can it ever be right to threaten to do something it would be wrong actually to do? 3. Do we have different standards for judging our enemy and ourselves? 4. Why is it right for us to have nuclear weapons, but wrong for Brazil, Israel, Pakistan and others? 5. Can the values we believe in ever be defended by nuclear weapons?' It was because the working party had unanimously come to believe that Christianity clearly implied the answers 'Yes, No, No, It isn't, and They can't be' that it felt the obligation to make its political recommendations. It became convinced that it is dangerous moonshine to suppose that the more powerful nuclear weapons could avoid inflicting massive civilian casualties, partly because 'military targets' are not 'isolated' from cities; and equally dangerous to suppose that the use of the smaller weapons would be likely to remain 'very restricted', partly because it is the official Soviet military doctrine that any use of tactical nuclear weapons by NATO would be followed by escalation into the use of strategic missiles and so into Doomsday.

Paul Johnson's article admitted these facts and seemed to agree that all nuclear weapons are so dreadful that it would never be right to use them. He therefore faced the crucial question: 'in order to prevent war, is it wrong to *threaten* to do something which if you *did* it would unquestionably be evil?' His answer was just as confused as anything in *The Church and the Bomb.* 'For the deterrent to succeed, and therefore retain its moral justification', he wrote, 'your opponent must believe that you not only *can* use it but in certain circumstances inevitably *will* use it, and to convey this belief it must reflect your real and manifest intention.' By way of defence of this 'unwanted and conditional evil in order to secure intended and unconditional good, the law of double effect may be invoked'. This was a reference to St Thomas Aquinas, who taught that moral acts take their character 'from what is intended and not what is beside the intention, since this is accidental'. But Paul Johnson was not wholly convinced. 'I confess', he wrote, 'there is no neat solution to this problem within the theological axis of the Just War doctrine.'

The authors of *The Church and the Bomb* found a solution: Christians must not commit *or threaten* evil. This solution was probably made easier for them by their belief that the USSR has no plans for the conquest of the world or even for the invasion of Western Europe; that it feels just as much encircled and threatened by the USA and its allies as the NATO countries are scared of the USSR. If this analysis of the political situation is correct, it becomes more tolerable to run risks by removing the threat to launch a nuclear war. That was why it seemed to this group right for Britain to set an example by renouncing nuclear weapons unilaterally. Of course it would be best if other countries imitated this step by deciding not to develop nuclear weapons, but it would still be right if no one did. They maintained that even if this step were to lead to the global imposition of communism, it would still remain sure that the values of the West should not be degraded by nuclear weapons – by using them, or by possessing them as a deterrent.

The purpose in bringing *The Church and the Bomb* to the General Synod was to test the reactions to such arguments of a sizeable body of bishops, clergy and laity. The debate was divided into two unequal sections. First came a general discussion of the principles, on a motion that the report should be 'received'. Only then did the Synod proceed to debate the controversial recommendations. This division of the subject was itself instructive. It reminded a great company of listeners, and many who were to read reports of the discussion, that the Church was attempting to reach a theological and spiritual agreement about the principles before getting entangled in the predictable disagreement about their application to British defence policy.

What seemed even stranger to many listeners and readers was the shape of each of these two debates, theological and political. Neither was introduced by Bishop Baker with an exposition of *The Church and the Bomb*. On the contrary, the first speaker in each section was the Bishop of London (Graham Leonard), who soon made clear how deeply he disagreed with much of the report. In terms of the procedure of the General Synod, this arrangement was due to the fact that *The Church and the Bomb* had been commissioned by the Board for Social Responsibility, whose chairman was Bishop Leonard. In terms of ecclesiastical politics, the acceptance of this procedure showed that the General Synod was by no means the bunch of pacifists or anarchists that had been haunting the imaginations of some overexcited journalists. The General Synod represented the Church of England, and the Bishop of London was in this position because he had commanded the confidence of many clergy and church-goers as a pastor and theologian with a definitely 'high church' or Anglo-Catholic background.

When dealing with political questions, he is probably best known for his insistence that the Church must not be identified with any political programme. The perfect Kingdom of God is for him not a Utopia to be brought about by the engineering of which politicians are capable; it is 'eternal fellowship with the living God, the Holy and the True, for which life in this world is a preparation'. He is usually firm about the moral ideals to be held before the Christian disciple as a soul in training for heaven – ideals which certainly include compassion and the duty to contribute to the improvement of society. But he is sceptical about some of the moral claims made to support political proposals. He stands out against a tendency, widespread among articulate twentieth-century Christians, to be permissive or at least tolerant about personal (for example, sexual) morality but firm on the necessity of radical actions to serve the causes of justice and peace in society. Before he rose in the debate in February 1983 he had become known as an outspoken critic of pacificism.

Opening the debate, he stressed: 'Though we differ as to how it is to be achieved, we must accept that we all desire the best for mankind, just as we must accept that we are all appalled at the horrifying prospect of nuclear war.' That acceptance held throughout the debate, which struck many listeners and readers as being more courteous and adult than the proceedings of the House of Commons. Dr Leonard also emphasised that 'the agonising dilemma of man today is that he is faced with the fact that the ultimate sanction for the enforcement of justice and the resistance to evil is of such a nature that it seems intolerable to contemplate its use.' Before the debate ended, he was to propose the official motion which declared that 'indiscriminate mass destruction in war cannot be justified in the light of Christian teaching'. This motion was carried without any recorded dissent. On the face of it, it ruled out any use by Britain of the Polaris missiles (each carrying three warheads with the destructive power of 200,000 tons of TNT and massive potential radiation) let alone the far more powerful Trident missiles. But Dr Leonard thought he was speaking for 'most, if not all, members' of his Board when he proceeded to criticise *The Church and the Bomb* for blurring the choice between renouncing nuclear weapons and possessing them in order to deter war. He quoted passages from the report which suggested that 'the bomb' would have a useful deterrent effect if left in American hands, but he hinted at the possibility that America might follow the British example and lamented that 'there is little consideration of how power is to be used in the pursuit of justice, particularly if the ultimate sanction is to be put in the hands of those who do not have justice in their vocabulary'.

The report's assessment of Soviet intentions was far too

optimistic; as Lenin had confessed, what peace meant was communist world domination and 'Leninist control means the repudiation of natural as well as Christian morality'. Dr Leonard preferred the Book of Revelation, with its 'vision of the defeat of evil portrayed in all its horror and with which there can be no compromise'. 'I believe', he ended, 'that we can only ask for and work for that fragile peace that is all that our sinfulness allows, that peace which deterrence gives, which recognises evil and seeks to check it while we repeat and call upon others to do the same in the hope that the Lord will give us what is better.'

In the theological debate, the Dean of Durham (Peter Baelz) set the tone by admitting to far more confusion than the Bishop of London had displayed. He believed that the use of nuclear weapons 'except perhaps on small tactical occasions' would be 'morally wrong' and that to threaten their use is 'morally corrupting and must be abjured as soon as possible'. Yet 'in the present situation it is right for the West to retain a nuclear deterrent' and it is 'justifiable' to include in this the threat of use. Other speakers did not get involved in the philosophical question about the morality of threats or of unintended acts. Nor (more curiously) did they make the point that deterrence requires not a certainty about the other side's response, but precisely *uncertainty* – a fact which slightly reduces the need to give the morally corruptive impression of complete certainty in willingness to inaugurate the obliteration of Soviet, American or British cities. But other speakers did press home some of the difficulties of such a threat for the Christian conscience. One spoke of the contrasting way of the cross taken by Jesus, another of a mother's feeling for the threatened creation, another of the agony of Hiroshima seen through the eyes of her Japanese son-in-law. Intellectually the Synod seemed to be arguing with the Bishop of London – and with Winston Churchill, who was quoted as declaring that 'until men's hearts are ruled by love they must be claimed by fear'. The Archbishop of York (Stuart Blanch) pointed out that nuclear weapons would never be disinvented, so that 'from now on every generation will be aware that it could be the last generation on earth'; and the only consolation he could offer was biblical. 'What is distinctive about the Christian attitude to the end of the world is that it is associated with joy and not just fear.' But the reactions of the Synod were expressed in applause for tributes to the quality of *The Church and the Bomb* – more generous tributes than any which the Bishop of London had produced. There was, it seemed, no feeling that the people of the Soviet Union deserved the horrors of the Apocalypse. Whatever might be true about their rulers, the people were not utterly evil nor blind to the difference between good and evil. And how would it be possible to strike at the rulers without striking at the people?

On behalf of his Board, Dr Leonard then moved a motion which called on the Government 'to reduce progressively its dependence upon nuclear weapons' and 'to work to strengthen international treaties'. He resented the description of this motion in the press as 'bland'. His Board was agreed that 'the present level of nuclear weapons is unnecessarily high' and in disarmament negotiations it was essential 'to take seriously all gestures which are made, even though the motives may be felt to be suspect'.

The subsequent debate began with speeches urging that the nuclear deterrent had maintained peace with a Soviet régime which was thoroughly evil, but the Bishop of Salisbury was at last called to present his report. He attacked 'the fallacy that mutual nuclear deterrence is a reasonably stable condition and likely to remain so'; the more accurate missiles become, the more powerful becomes the temptation to strike first. He attacked, too, 'our second fallacy: defence demands parity'. Since 'both East and West have many times more weapons than they need for deterrence', either side could make unilateral cuts without jeopardising its security; and while 'pure total unilateralism by the West' is 'fantasy', the phasing out of Britain's share ('no more than five per cent') would be a 'safe initiative' intended 'to stimulate general disarmament'. In this speech Bishop Baker did not do himself justice – or so many were saying afterwards. It was his

maiden speech to the Synod; he was nervous. And it was
political; he was not on his home ground as a theologian. He
underestimated the effect which a British refusal to have
anything to do with nuclear weapons would have on NATO
and did not tackle the question: Would our hands be really
clean if we still relied on the Americans? His political predic-
tions were open to the reply which they received.

The Archbishop of Canterbury's interventions in General
Synod debates often carry the day. This time Dr Runcie
distanced himself from any enthusiasm for the nuclear deterrent: 'We are talking about a world that is in the grip of
madness.' He advocated 'more immediate resort to the
Security Council and the building up of the UN policing
capability', and he deplored the growing trade in arms. But
he did not want Britain to send any 'misleading signals to
those who have been tempted to pursue aggression'. (Previous speakers had reminded the Synod that such signals had
been sent to Argentina before its invasion of the Falklands.)
He believed that the adoption of the recommendations in *The
Church and the Bomb* would seem 'a repudiation of the
cornerstone of NATO's defence policy' and would strain 'the
alliance on which the peace and stability of Europe has rested
since World War II'. And he believed it 'most improbable'
that it would bring in any new signatory to the Non-
Proliferation Treaty. 'I do not impugn the honesty or good
faith of those who support unilateralism, but I believe there is
also moral seriousness in the multilateral approach.' And it
was the approach he thought best.

Multilateral disarmament was the approach which in the
end the Synod blessed, rejecting the Bishop of Salisbury's
amendment to the official motion by 338 votes to 100. And
the authors of *The Church and the Bomb* were probably not
surprised by this evidence of loyalty to NATO. General Sir
Hugh Beach put his finger on the flaw which they had
themselves built into their recommendations. 'The truth', he
wrote after the debate, 'is that they seek nuclear disarmament
for its own sake, in pursuit of what they believe to be the
Christian decision. Dodging the logic, they seek to apply this

precept to Britain, and Britain alone, because to do so more widely would be – as they accurately perceive – highly dangerous.' But as the debate continued that February afternoon it became clear that the Synod did indeed agree with some journalists that the official motion's commendation of multilateralism was too bland. An MP who later that year was to become Chairman of the Conservative Party (John Selwyn Gummer) defended against some of his colleagues the Church's right to discuss such questions; 'if ever there were a matter on which we have something special to say it is this'. While advocating multilateralism, he showed no complacency about the present balance of terror between the superpowers. The goal must be 'disarmament for the whole world' and 'I feel deeply that Christians of all people must attempt the impossible'.

The Bishop of Birmingham (Hugh Montefiore) opened up for the Synod a way of combining the multilateral approach with a more definite – if still perhaps 'impossible' – first step which NATO could take on its own: the pledge about nuclear weapons of 'no first use'. It is curious that this outcome of the debate was not included among the recommendations in *The Church and the Bomb*; it was not even discussed there as a possibility. But Bishop Montefiore is an eloquent speaker who can think on his feet, partly because he worked for many years in Cambridge before moving to South London and Birmingham and has thought closely about social questions. Later in 1983 he took over the chairmanship of the Board for Social Responsibility from Bishop Leonard. And now he won the day.

On the one hand, he argued that deterrence, including nuclear deterrence against aggression, 'is a positive duty of the State'. 'To use it would be catastrophic and immoral,' he admitted. But 'if it is effective, it will deter, and so never be used. That is the justification.' And 'if one side lacked the deterrent, this would make nuclear war far more likely'; indeed, 'it seems to me – but I may be wrong – that the planet will go on needing a nuclear deterrent to the end of time to guard against nuclear blackmail'. To questions about the ethics of the State, 'there are no direct answers from the New Testament, because there we find only the ethics of personal action'. On the other hand, 'what is needed is a solemn assurance believed in by both sides, given by both sides, that they will never indulge in "first use" or "first strike". This frees everyone at a stroke from nuclear black-mail and nuclear aggression.'

The next speaker was more cautious; 'there are certain situations in a conventional war where we would have either to surrender or use a nuclear weapon'. The Bishop of London voiced the same objections. 'I should like to ask the Bishop of Birmingham what he would actually do in the event of attack by conventional weapons on NATO forces which threatened to overrun them completely.' When his fellow-bishop had replied that 'if I were to give advice to the commander-in-chief, which I would not, I could not advise him first use of a new type of dreadful weapon', Dr Leonard warned: 'if you are going to have any form of deterrence, then you cannot in advance say you will not use it'. But the Synod was in no mood to regard the difficulties of NATO commanders as decisive. It did not feel any duty to explore such questions as whether taxes should be raised, or social services cut, or conscription restored in Britain, in order to strengthen NATO's non-nuclear defences. This is a policy which seems possible (the Supreme Commander of NATO has urged it) but expensive. The Synod was not minded to count the cost. Nor was it eager to listen to the more fundamental – and opposing – convictions of the Chaplain of the Fleet and the Church's leading pacifist (Paul Oestreicher), who were called late in the debate. By this time the Bishop of Salisbury's amendment was clearly going to be lost, and the nail was driven into its coffin by the Bishop of Durham (John Habgood). 'What the world would see', he claimed, 'would not be a highly moral gesture but yet further evidence of British decline.' The Synod was looking round for a way of lessening the nuclear risks without wrecking NATO – and the Bishop of Birmingham seemed to have provided it.

His amendment was carried by 275 votes to 222, and the

official motion incorporating it attracted 387 votes against 49 with 29 abstentions. Thus the Synod affirmed that 'it is the duty of Her Majesty's Government and her allies to maintain adequate forces to guard against nuclear blackmail and to deter nuclear and non-nuclear aggressors'. This did not necessarily mean endorsing the modernisation of Britain's independent deterrent; earlier in the debate Bishop Montefiore had himself remarked that 'I think Trident Mark 2 is a dreadful waste of money'. But the successful motion failed to condemn Trident (or Polaris) – or to rule out the second use of nuclear weapons. It did not prophesy against the possession of the nuclear deterrent as the World Council of Churches had done, nor qualify its toleration as the Pope had done. It made the *Daily Mirror* headline inevitable: 'Church backs the Bomb'.

However, this support for deterrence was balanced by the repetition from the earlier official motion of the plea that since 'nuclear parity is not essential to deterrence', NATO's dependence on nuclear weapons should be 'reduced progressively', together with 'nuclear arsenals throughout the world'. The strong endorsement of deterrence was also balanced by a new declaration that 'there is a moral obligation on all countries publicly to forswear the first use of nuclear weapons in any form'. And that echo of the teaching of (for example) the American Catholic bishops pleased Conservatives less. It was a view, said the *Daily Telegraph*, 'formed with a complete disregard for technical realities'. The Soviet Union had offered just such a pledge of no first use, but the newly-appointed Secretary of State for Defence, Michael Heseltine, quickly rejected it as 'a self-evident piece of propaganda'. Commenting on the Synod's resolution, he argued that for NATO to rule out the option of a nuclear response 'would be to invite the Russians to launch a conventional war' since the Soviets had 'massive conventional forces' and believed that if they attacked with these, with no risk of nuclear deterrence, 'they would win'.

The *Daily Telegraph* and Michael Heseltine were perhaps too gloomy about the prospects of a sustainable defence in the

new age of military technology, but their wrath was a re-
minder of the probable attitude of Western electorates when
asked to foot the bill for what might become a conventional
arms race. And in *Crucible*, the journal of the Board for Social
Responsibility (April–June 1983), the Dean of King's College, London (Richard Harries), also condemned the idea as
increasing the risk of war. 'The prime moral duty is to avoid
war, for if war broke out there is no likelihood that it could be
brought to a slithering halt at the nuclear firebreak.' He
quoted the Socialist President of France, M. Mitterand:
'What we seek is the prevention of war, and that can be
guaranteed only by nuclear deterrence.' Thus moral as well
as military objections might be raised. The authors of *The
Church and the Bomb* had themselves issued the warning:
'There are no simple solutions to the problems created by
nuclear weapons, no risk-free policies, no courses of action
which allow us to escape from ethical dilemmas.'

So should Christians attempt the impossible, or at least
hold up a vision of sanity in a world gripped by madness?
'Multilateralists must be greatly encouraged by the fact that
the Synod result was achieved after a debate of considerable
quality and distinction', the *Yorkshire Post* wrote editorially
(under the headline 'Church redeemed'). The Prime Minister was reported as thinking the debate 'marvellous'. But the
Observer noticed that the Synod 'gave its longest and warmest
applause to the loser, the Bishop of Salisbury; and it quoted
Mgr Bruce Kent of the Campaign for Nuclear Disarmament
as saying that 'the vote was a good step towards limiting
nuclear risk. If implemented it would have a radical effect on
NATO's present policies.' Unilateralists were not downcast
by the fact that less than a third of the Synod voted for their
complete programmes for Britain; on the contrary, many
were impressed by the seriousness with which their case had
been treated. Many tributes were paid to the integrity,
intelligence, knowledgeability and courtesy shown in the
debate, probably the General Synod's most glorious hour.
But many felt that further studies must be made, further
thought devoted to the complexities, a deeper dedication

given to the ultimate simplicity. A Yorkshire vicar (Peter Mullen) contributed to the *Guardian* a dream about the Lord coming to Westminster and declaring: 'Cast out first the megatons which are in thine own arsenal and then thou shalt see clearly to cast out the megatons that are in thine enemy's . . . Behold thine enemy, that he also hath kinsfolk and children. And are there not strangers within his gate which also are without guile and innocent of great offence? Wouldst thou destroy them . . . ? Love thine enemies.'

Early in the General Synod's debate a speaker commented that it seemed impossible to bring together the world of the Church, which was or ought to be a world under the cross, and the world of the bomb. But the debate continues. Later in 1983 three other sophisticated collections of essays were published developing or contradicting points made in the Synod.[3] In church gatherings, homes, offices and pubs, the more informal arguments have been unending. No one can say that Christians are indifferent. It may be that, having already condemned indiscriminate mass destruction in war, they are about to form a stronger consensus on the morality of the possession and use of nuclear weapons large and small. Or it may be that in addition to prayer as the highest expression of concern, the great debate is all that the Church as a body can usefully contribute to a world dominated by these satanic instruments of death which are also widely believed to be the pillars of peace.

---

1 *The Church and The Bomb*, Church of England Board for Social Responsibility (Hodder & Stoughton, 1982).
2 Robinson, John A. T., *Honest to God* (SCM 1963).
3 Harries, Richard (ed), *What Hope in an Armed World?* (Pickering & Inglis, 1982) gathered experts, all but one associated with King's College, London.
Bridger, Francis (ed), *The Cross and the Bomb* (Mowbray & Co., 1983) discussed the moral case for multilateralism.
Martin, David & Mullen, Peter (eds), *Unholy Warfare* (Blackwell, 1983) covered the widest possible spectrum.

Section II

WEAPONS AND STRATEGIES

2 WILL THERE BE A NUCLEAR WAR?
Frank Barnaby

Few would question that a nuclear world war is the greatest single threat to our society, if not to humankind. Many believe that the probability of a nuclear world war is steadily increasing. And that a, if not the, major reason for this increasing probability is that the nuclear arms race between the USA and the USSR is out of political control. Only if, and when, this arms race is brought under control, will the danger of a nuclear holocaust begin to recede. It is, therefore, crucially important to understand the nature of the super-power nuclear arms race and to try to fathom the causes of it.

The nuclear weapons now in the arsenals of the nuclear-weapon powers have a vast range of explosive power – varying between the equivalent of 10 tons of TNT and at least twenty million tons (twenty megatons). It is hard to appreciate what destructive power a twenty-megaton nuclear war-head has. It might help to know that the total weight of all the explosives used by man in war throughout history is roughly twenty megatons. Yes, the superpowers really do have nuclear warheads each of which contains as much explosive power as *all the explosives used in war so far put together*.

Nuclear Weapons
Nuclear warheads are of two types – strategic and tactical. Range is the main distinguishing factor between them, the former having very long (intercontinental) ranges, greater than say 6,000 kilometres. But the existence of intermediate range missiles, like SS-20 and Cruise, confuses the distinction between different types of weapon.

a) Strategic nuclear weapons are deployed on intercontinental ballistic missiles (ICBMs), submarine-launched ballistic missiles (SLBMs), and strategic bombers. Soviet and American ICBMs have ranges of about 11,000 kilometres, modern SLBMs have ranges of about 7,000 kilometres, and strategic bombers have ranges of about 12,000 kilometres.

Some ballistic missiles carry many warheads – up to fourteen. Modern multiple warheads are independently targetable on targets hundreds of kilometres apart. These are called multiple independently-targetable re-entry vehicles, or MIRVs in shorthand.

Strategic bombers carry free-fall nuclear bombs and air-to-ground missiles armed with nuclear warheads. The most modern of these missiles is the American air-launched Cruise missile (ALCM) carried by the B-52 strategic bomber; the ALCM has a range of about 2,500 kilometres.

The USA has (end, 1983) 1,613 strategic ballistic missiles – 1,045 ICBMs and 568 SLBMs. Of these, 1,118 (568 SLBMs and 550 ICBMs) are fitted with MIRVs. Two hundred and seventy-four B-52s are operational as strategic bombers, carrying 1,096 nuclear free-fall bombs; 1,020 short-range attack missiles with nuclear warheads; and 384 ALCMs.

These American strategic nuclear forces carry about 9,800 nuclear warheads – 2,100 on ICBMs, 5,200 on SLBMs and 2,500 on bombers. These warheads can deliver a total explosive power of 4,200 megatons (Mt); 1,400 by ICBMs, 400 by SLBMs and 2,400 by bombers.

The USSR has (end, 1983) 2,339 strategic ballistic missiles – 1,398 ICBMs and 941 SLBMs. Of these, 1,032 (244 SLBMs and 788 ICBMs) could be fitted with MIRVs. Some 140 Soviet long-range bombers may be assigned an intercontinental strategic role.

These Soviet strategic nuclear forces carry about 7,700 warheads on ballistic missiles – about 5,600 on ICBMs, 1,800 on SLBMs, and perhaps 300 on bombers. These warheads can deliver about 6,000 Mt, about 5,000 by ICBM,

700 by SLBM, and 300 by bombers. The bombers may carry free-fall bombs and short-range attack missiles.

b) *Tactical nuclear weapons* are deployed in a wide variety of systems – including howitzer and artillery shells, ground-to-ground ballistic missiles, free-fall bombs, air-to-ground missiles, anti-aircraft missiles, atomic demolition munitions (land-mines), ground-, air-, and submarine-launched Cruise missiles, torpedoes, naval mines, depth charges, and anti-submarine rockets. Land-based tactical systems have ranges varying from about 12 kilometres or less (artillery shells) to a few thousand kilometres (intermediate range ballistic missiles). The explosive power of tactical nuclear warheads varies from about 10 tons to about 1 Mt.

The USA deploys tactical nuclear weapons in Western Europe, Asia, and the United States, and with the Atlantic and Pacific fleets. The USSR deploys its tactical nuclear weapons in Eastern Europe.

Nuclear arsenals

Data on nuclear-weapon stockpiles are crucial for an informed debate on nuclear-weapon issues. Much information about the nuclear arsenals of other nuclear-weapon powers has been made publicly available by American intelligence agencies. Available public information about American nuclear stockpiles has been recently collated by the American scientists W. M. Arkin, T. B. Cochran, and M. M. Hoenig in a *Nuclear Weapons Data Book* (Ballinger, 1983).

1. USA

Considerable changes are planned in the US nuclear arsenal over the next ten years. The deployment of new weapons is changing policies from nuclear deterrence based on mutual assured destruction to nuclear-war fighting. Further deployments are likely to stimulate even more far-reaching changes – specifically to nuclear war-winning policies.

Currently, according to Arkin et al., the US nuclear arsenal contains about 26,000 nuclear weapons – down from the peak of some 32,000 reached in 1967. Today's weapons

are spread over twenty-five types – ranging from portable
land-mines, weighing a mere 70 kilograms to strategic
bombs, weighing about 3.6 tons. As we have seen, the
explosive power of the weapons varies considerably – from
the equivalent of about 10 tons of TNT for the W54 atomic
land-mine to that of 9 million tons of TNT for the B-53
strategic bomb. Twelve types of US nuclear weapons are
currently deployed in NATO countries.

The numbers of nuclear weapons of different types in the
US stockpile vary considerably. The numbers range from
3,500 for the W48 155 mm nuclear artillery shell to 65 for the
W53 Titan II ICBM warhead. The numbers of nuclear
free-fall aircraft bombs deployed total about 7,500, spread
over five types.

The number of tactical nuclear weapons (about 16,000) is
approaching the number of strategic nuclear weapons
(roughly 10,000) – a change from the 1950s and 1960s when
the US stockpile was mainly tactical. About 6,000 tactical
nuclear warheads are deployed in NATO.

The likelihood is that the US will deploy 23,000 new
nuclear warheads by the end of the 1980s. Making an allow-
ance for the fact that about 17,000 warheads will be with-
drawn from the stockpile, or replaced during this time, the
number of nuclear warheads will grow from the current
26,000 to 32,000 by 1990 – the number will, in other words,
grow back to the previous all-time record reached in 1967.

2. USSR
The Soviet nuclear arsenal is about the same size as the
American one. This means that together the superpowers
have deployed about 45,000 nuclear weapons. For comparison, the nuclear arsenals of the other established nuclear-
weapon powers (the UK, France and China) contain a total of
about 2,500 nuclear warheads. The total explosive power of
the American and Soviet nuclear arsenals is roughly 16,000
Mt – equivalent to over one million Hiroshima bombs, or to
over 3 tons of TNT to every man, woman, and child on earth,
or to 750 times all the high explosive used in all the wars in

history. The nuclear arsenals are now, and have for many years been, much larger than needed for any conceivable military, political or strategic reason.

Because of the amount of 'overkill' in the nuclear arsenals, further increases in numbers of nuclear weapons deployed are much less important than qualitative improvements in the weapons themselves. It is the qualitative developments which are causing changes in nuclear policies.

The most important qualitative advances in nuclear weapons are those which improve the accuracy, reliability and targeting flexibility of nuclear weapon systems. Many types of new weapon will be seen as suitable for fighting a nuclear war but not suitable for deterring a nuclear war by mutual assured destruction. Very accurate ballistic missiles can deliver warheads over intercontinental ranges on smaller – and therefore many more – military targets than less accurate ones. In fact, with extremely accurate and reliable nuclear weapons the perception will grow on one side or the other that it will be possible to destroy the enemy's retaliatory capability by striking first.

It is not necessary for one side to possess the ability completely to destroy the other side's retaliatory capability for such a first strike to be contemplated. It is sufficient for the attacker to believe (or perceive) that a surprise attack will reduce the enemy's capability to retaliate to the point where the attacker's casualties, caused by the retaliatory attack, will be 'acceptable' for a given political goal.

In this context one must remember that, in times of crisis, political leaders are more apt to listen to the advice of their military chiefs than to their civilian scientific advisers. The calculations of casualties which affect military decisions are likely to be based on wrong assumptions about the military performance of both sides: the performance of the enemy's weapons are likely to be overestimated and those on our side underestimated; worst case analysis for our performance and best case analysis for theirs. Also the calculations about the effects of nuclear weapons are likely to emphasise estimates of prompt deaths and injuries and ignore the uncertain long-term effects, even though these long-term effects may well ultimately be more lethal. In addition, the serious sociological and psychological consequences of the total loss of social and technical services and the trauma of nuclear war are likely to be ignored.

Modernisation of nuclear weapons

The accuracy of a nuclear weapon is normally measured by the circular error probability (CEP), the radius of the circle centred on the target, within which half of a large number of warheads fired at the target will fall. In both the USA and the USSR, the CEPs of ballistic missiles, ICBMs and SLBMs, and of tactical nuclear weapons are being continually improved.

1. USA

In the USA, for example, improvements have been made in the guidance system of the Minuteman III ICBM to reduce the CEP of the Minuteman III to about 200 metres. At the same time the design of the Minuteman warhead has been improved so that its explosive power has increased from 170,000 tons (170 kt) of TNT equivalent to 330 kt.

The new Minuteman III warheads delivered with the higher accuracy could destroy Soviet ICBMs in their silos with a probability of success of about 57 per cent for one shot and about 95 per cent for two shots.

The improved land-based ICBM force significantly increases US nuclear-war fighting capabilities. These will be further increased by the MX missile system now under development which is expected to have a CEP of about 100 metres.

2. USSR

The most formidable of Soviet ICBMs is the SS-18. This is thought to have a CEP of about 400 or 500 metres, with the accuracy soon being improved to about 250 metres. Each SS-18 warhead probably has an explosive power of about 500 kt. With the higher accuracy a typical SS-18 warhead would

have about a 55 per cent chance of destroying a US Minuteman ICBM in its silo. Two warheads fired in succession
would have about a 95 per cent chance of success.

The USSR also has the SS-19 ICBM, which is thought to
be somewhat more accurate than the SS-18 and equipped
with a similar warhead. Some of both the SS-18s and SS-19s
are MIRVed, the missiles carrying six, eight or ten warheads.
In one of the single-warhead versions, the SS-18 is thought to
carry a 20 Mt warhead, which is probably the world's biggest.

The other Soviet MIRVed ICBM, the SS-17, carries four
warheads, each with an explosive power of 750 kt. The Soviet
MIRVed ICBM force may carry a total of nearly 5,000
warheads. The US MIRVed ICBM force carries 1,650 warheads.

The Soviet strategic ICBM force is an increasing threat to
the 1,000-strong US Minuteman ICBM force, as the accuracy
and reliability of the Soviet warheads are improved. On both
sides, the land-based ballistic missile forces provide a
nuclear-war fighting element in the nuclear policies, in that
the land-based missiles are increasingly targeted on small
hardened military targets. The submarine-based strategic
forces, however, still provide an element of nuclear deterrence by mutual assured destruction.

Strategic nuclear submarines

The Soviet and American navies operate a total of ninety-six
modern strategic nuclear submarines, equipped with
SLBMs. The ballistic missiles carried by submarines are
normally targeted on the enemy's cities and industry, and
provide the assured destruction on which nuclear deterrence
currently depends. A single US strategic nuclear submarine,
for example, carries about 200 warheads, enough to destroy
every Soviet city with a population of more than 150,000
people. American cities are hostages to Soviet strategic nuclear submarines to the same extent as Soviet cities are to
American strategic submarines. Just four strategic submarines on appropriate stations in the oceans could destroy
most of the major cities in the Northern Hemisphere.

1. USSR

The most modern operational class of Soviet ballistic missile submarine is the Delta class, carrying twelve or sixteen SLBMs, the missiles having ranges of about 8,000 kilometres. The SS-N-18, the missile carried by Delta-class submarines, is the first Soviet SLBM to be MIRVed. These missiles could hit most targets in the USA from Soviet home waters.

In 1980, the USSR launched a very large strategic nuclear submarine, the Typhoon. This 160-metre boat displaces, when submerged, 25,000 tons and carries twenty SLBMs. It will become operational in about the mid-1980s and be equipped with a new, more accurate ballistic missile, the SS-NX-20. This SLBM will probably carry twelve warheads over a range of about 8,000 kilometres.

By the end of 1983, the USSR had deployed 941 SLBMs, 244 of them MIRVed, in its sixty-two strategic nuclear submarines. These SLBMs are capable of delivering about 800 nuclear warheads, about 24 per cent of the total number of warheads in the Soviet nuclear arsenal.

2. USA AND NATO

The USA now operates two types of SLBM – the Poseidon and the Trident I. Each Poseidon carries, on average, nine MIRVs, each with a yield of 40 kt; each Trident I carries, on average, eight MIRVs, each with a yield of 100 kt.

Trident I SLBMs are deployed on Trident submarines and on Poseidon submarines. The Tridents are new boats. Two are now in operation. They are approximately twice as large as the Poseidon missile submarines which they are replacing. Each Trident carries twenty-four Trident SLBMs, with ranges of about 7,500 kilometres. Seven more Trident submarines are being built. They should become operational at the rate of about one a year.

Trident I SLBMs are being retro-fitted into Poseidon strategic nuclear submarines. So far, twelve Poseidons have been fitted with the new ballistic missiles. Nineteen other

Poseidon boats are operational; each carrying sixteen Poseidon missiles, with ranges of about 4,500 kilometres.

The extra range of the Trident SLBMs allows the submarines carrying them to operate in much larger areas of the oceans and still be within range of targets in the USSR. The submarines do not then have to expose themselves to the same extent to Soviet anti-submarine warfare systems.

The US Navy can operate 568 SLBMs carrying a total of about 5,200 warheads, with a total explosive power of about 400 Mt. Nearly 50 per cent of American strategic nuclear warheads are carried on submarines.

Strategic Bombers

1. USA

The USA is continually modernising its strategic bomber fleet. Currently, B-52s are being provided with air-launched Cruise missiles (ALCMs); the plan is to deploy some 3,000 Cruise missiles, twenty-five per bomber. The Reagan Administration also plans to build 100 B-1B bombers to replace some of the ageing B-52s. The first B-1Bs should be operational in 1986 and they will also carry ALCMs. The Administration is also encouraging intensive research into the Advanced Technology Bomber, or 'Stealth' aircraft. This programme involves the development of radar-absorbing materials and aircraft shapes to give a very small radar cross-section, as well as terrain-following and other systems to avoid detection by Soviet air-defence systems.

The ALCM is a long-range, subsonic nuclear-armed winged vehicle, about 6 metres long, weighing less than 1,360 kilograms, with a range of about 2,500 kilometres, and a nuclear warhead of about 200 kt. The ALCMs could be launched outside Soviet territory against air defence systems, to destroy their radar and anti-aircraft missiles. Following B-52s would then be able to penetrate into Soviet territory to attack targets with their nuclear bombs and ALCMs. The missiles are accurate enough to be used against small, hardened military targets and because they have relatively small radar cross-sections are difficult to detect by radars on the ground.

2. USSR

Unlike the USA, the USSR maintains an extensive air defence system based on a family of surface-to-air missiles and a large number of interceptor aircraft. The Soviets will probably extend their air-defence system to be able to cope with the Cruise missiles now being deployed by the USA. This will probably involve deploying Airborne Warning and Control System aircraft constantly to patrol the Soviet borders to detect incoming air- or ground-launched Cruise missiles, and alert and control fighter aircraft and surface-to-air missiles to shoot down the enemy missiles. There are those who believe that the main reason for the deployment by the USA of Cruise missiles is to provoke the USSR into spending large sums on counter-measures.

Modernisation of tactical nuclear weapons

Both the USA and the USSR are modernising their tactical nuclear arsenals.

Among the new types of nuclear weapon being deployed in NATO are Pershing II missiles and ground-launched Cruise missiles. These weapons are so accurate as to be perceived as nuclear-war fighting weapons; both have a CEP of about 50 metres. Although less accurate than the American missiles, the Soviet SS-20, an intermediate range ballistic missile, is accurate enough, or soon will be made so, to be a nuclear war-fighting weapon, given the relatively large explosive power of its warhead.

The Soviet SS-20, first deployed in 1976, is a two-stage mobile missile, with a range of about 5,000 kilometres. About 400 of the missiles are deployed (early 1984) in the USSR; about 60 per cent are targeted on Western Europe (from sites West of the Urals) and the rest on China and possible other Asian targets (from sites East of the Urals). Each SS-20 normally carries three MIRVed warheads, each with a yield said to be about 150 kt. The CEP of the SS-20 is thought to be about 800 metres.

The Pershing II, replacing the Pershing I missiles deployed in West Germany, will be provided with a sophisticated new guidance system called RADAG. When the warhead approaches its target a video radar scans the target area and the image is compared with a reference image stored in the warhead's computer before the missile is launched. The computer controls aerodynamic vanes which guide the warhead on to its target with an accuracy unprecedented in a missile with a range of 1,800 kilometres. The missile, due for deployment from the end of 1983, will be the only ballistic missile able to penetrate a significant distance into the USSR; it could, for example, reach Moscow from its sites in West Germany. The plan is to deploy 108 Pershing IIs with warheads having yields in the low kilotonnage range.

NATO plans to deploy 464 ground-launched Cruise missiles between 1984 and 1988, in West Germany, Italy, the UK, Belgium, and the Netherlands. The missiles will have ranges of about 2,500 kilometres and carry warheads with a yield in the kiloton range.

The USSR is now deploying new missile systems in Eastern Europe, with nuclear warheads targeted on West Germany, Italy and the UK. The new Soviet tactical nuclear missiles include the SS-21 (with a maximum range of about 120 kilometres); the SS-22 (with a maximum range of about 1,000 kilometres); and the SS-23 (with a maximum range of about 500 kilometres).

From nuclear deterrence to nuclear war-fighting to nuclear war-winning

Until the end of the 1970s the nuclear policy of the USA was nuclear deterrence by mutual assured destruction. Nuclear deterrence depends on the belief that the enemy will not attack suddenly (pre-emptively) if he knows that most of his cities and industry will be destroyed in retaliation. If the enemy no longer fears that his cities are at risk nuclear deterrence by mutual assured destruction no longer works

This is precisely what happens when accurate and reliable weapons are deployed.

Deterrence is essentially a matter of psychology. What matters is what the enemy believes. It is impossible to maintain a policy of nuclear deterrence by mutual assured destruction with accurate weapons simply because the enemy will assume, willy-nilly, that the other side's nuclear warheads are targeted on his military forces and not on his cities. The cities then cease to be the hostages. Accuracy, in other words, kills deterrence. Nuclear-war fighting based on the destruction of hostile military forces, then becomes the only credible, and therefore feasible, policy.

War-fighting deterrence, as it has been called, is giving way to war-winning strategies, in which it is argued that victory is possible in a nuclear war. Typical advocates of the possibility of nuclear victory are Colin Gray and Keith Payne, two American strategists. In a nuclear war, they argue, 'the United States should plan to defeat the Soviet Union and to do so at a cost that would not prohibit US recovery'. They go on, 'a combination of counterforce offensive targeting, civil defence, and ballistic missile and air defense should hold US casualties down to a level compatible with national survival and recovery'.

Over the next six year period, 1983–8, the US Administration plans to spend about $450,000 million on modernising and improving the American nuclear arsenal. A range of military technologies are being developed which will strengthen nuclear-war fighting and winning perceptions. The most important are those related to anti-submarine warfare, anti-ballistic missiles, and anti-satellite warfare systems.

If one side could severely limit the damage that the other side's strategic nuclear submarines could do in a retaliatory strike, and believed that it could destroy – by, for example, high-energy lasers in space – any enemy missile warheads which survived a surprise attack, then the temptation to make an all-out first strike may become wellnigh irresistible, particularly during a period of international crisis.

Out of Control?

Many believe that the progression from nuclear deterrence by mutual assured destruction to nuclear-war fighting to nuclear-war winning, is considerably increasing the danger of a nuclear world war. We have seen that this situation is coming about mainly because the nuclear arms race is continually producing qualitative improvements in nuclear weapons and their supporting technologies. Even if political leaders wanted to maintain their old policy of nuclear deterrence by mutual assured destruction they would be prevented from doing so by the characteristics of the new nuclear weapons developed by military scientists.

Today, about 500,000 scientists work only on military research and development, about 25 per cent of all scientists employed on research. This large group of scientists is a powerful political lobby. Moreover, vast bureaucracies have grown up in the great powers to deal with military matters. Academics and bureaucrats join with the military and the weapons industry to form a giant academic-bureaucratic-military-industrial complex intent on maintaining and increasing military budgets and agitating for the use of every conceivable technological advance for military purposes. This complex has so much political power as to be almost politically irresistible. If this is so, the nuclear arms race is now totally out of the control of political leaders. And this is as true in the Soviet Union as it is in the USA.

In fact, because similar military technological developments are taking place in the USSR, Soviet and American nuclear policies must be expected to develop in roughly the same way. In most areas of military technology the USA is ahead of the USSR but the gap is only a few years. The knowledge that the other side will catch up will increase the temptation to make a surprise nuclear attack once the perception of a first-strike capability develops.

Conclusions

I believe that the above evidence leads to the following conclusions:

1. The nuclear arms race is out of political control.

2. Unless the nuclear arms race is soon brought under control there will be a nuclear catastrophe.

3. Nuclear weapons now being developed and deployed are accurate and reliable enough to be seen as suitable for fighting a nuclear war but useless for deterring nuclear war by mutual assured destruction. Currently, superpower nuclear policy is a rather confused (and confusing) mixture of nuclear-war fighting and nuclear deterrence by mutual assured destruction.

4. After another five years, when SLBMs are nuclear-war fighting, superpower nuclear strategies will be pure nuclear-war fighting; nuclear deterrence by mutual assured destruction will be dead.

5. When anti-submarine warfare, anti-ballistic missile, and anti-satellite warfare systems are available, in say fifteen years' time, the perception of a first-strike will be possible and, therefore, probable; nuclear-war winning strategies may then dominate.

6. The worst situation would be the deployment of nuclear-war fighting weapons in Europe together with nuclear-war fighting strategic weapons in the superpowers.

7. To reduce these dangers it is necessary:

   a) to prevent the modernisation of nuclear weapons in Europe;

   b) this means, in practice, to remove nuclear weapons from the landmass of Europe, because if nuclear weapons are deployed their modernisation is inevitable;

   c) to encourage the superpowers to scrap their ICBMs and strategic bombers, which are now so vulnerable as to be obsolete; this would effectively mean reliance on strategic nuclear submarines and a return to mutual assured destruction;

   d) the submarines should then be reduced in number, eventually to zero, as their ballistic missiles become nuclear-war fighting weapons.

8. This programme of nuclear disarmament should be incorporated into a comprehensive disarmament pro-

gramme, including a comprehensive permanent ban on nuclear-weapons tests, bans on chemical weapons, control of offensive conventional weapons, control of the global arms trade and the spread of nuclear weapons, and so on.

9. This disarmament programme will only be achieved if the pressure of public opinion is strong enough to overcome the pressure exerted on the political leaders by the military-industrial-academic-bureaucratic complex.

10. To mobilise public opinion it will be necessary to present alternative defence policies to the current policies which rely on the first and early use of nuclear weapons.

11. To avoid the further escalation of the arms race, such an alternative defence policy should be non-nuclear and non-provocative.

12. In a period of low economic growth, the alternative policy should cost no more than current military budgets.

13. Using available and imminent conventional defensive technologies a non-provocative, non-nuclear, militarily-credible, defensive deterrent is possible.

14. The choice for Europe is war or no war because any war in Europe will almost certainly escalate to an all-out strategic nuclear war, whether or not nuclear weapons are deployed in Europe.

15. A non-nuclear, non-provocative defence posture would minimise the probability of a war in Europe.

For Discussion

1. Do you think the nuclear arms race is out of control?

2. What practical steps could be taken to mobilise public opinion as suggested by Frank Barnaby?

3. Has the Church a role in mobilising opinion?

3 MILITARY IMPLICATIONS OF 'NO FIRST USE'
General Sir Hugh Beach

'Non-nuclear cruise missiles for the RAF'. This headline, covered a report that Britain, West Germany and the USA are jointly to develop a non-nuclear air to ground missile, with a range of several hundred kilometres, for use with the Tornado aircraft against enemy airfields and other fixed targets. It appeared in *The Times* on October 22nd, 1983, the very day of the great demonstrations planned against the deployment of nuclear Cruise missiles in Western Europe. Whether coincidentally or not, the emergence of a non-nuclear version of Cruise signals a revolutionary change in the thinking of defence planners about the role of nuclear weapons in the defence of Western Europe. Admiral Falls, the outgoing chairman of NATO's Military Committee, in his valedictory remarks in June 1983, spoke clearly of the need to act – if necessary unilaterally – to reduce battlefield nuclear weapons. General Rogers, Supreme Allied Commander in Europe, has for more than a year been preaching the merit of an enhanced non-nuclear defence. 'We must and can strengthen our conventional forces so that they are not a *de facto* tripwire for nuclear escalation . . . We can reduce the possibility of a (Warsaw) Pact attack by establishing the *credible prospect that our conventional defence will succeed*' (my italics).[1]

So for the first time we have prominent NATO commanders publicly joining hands with those whose Christian conscience enjoins them, to work for the removal of the existing NATO doctrine, whereby the West plans to initiate a nuclear war if it was attacked by the Warsaw Pact countries and was otherwise in danger of being overwhelmed. The ethical case for a policy of 'no first use' has been argued in other chapters of this book. This chapter seeks to explore the military implications in the light of 'Emerging Technology' – an unlovely jargon phrase quaintly abbreviated to ET.

The nuclear weapons presently available for battlefield use in the defence of Western Europe are said to consist of some 500 warheads for surface-to-surface missiles with ranges from 70 to 700 kilometres; about 2,000 free-falling bombs for fighter-bomber aircraft, including the British Jaguar, Buccaneer and Tornado; much the same number of shells for self-propelled artillery, and about 300 nuclear land-mines. The vast majority of the warheads are American in origin, and remain at all times in American custody and control, at 'special ammunition sites' in Western Germany. In many cases, however, the 'delivery means' – guns, missiles and aircraft – have been sold to allies and are then wholly operated by them. This arrangement means that the nuclear warhead in question can only be fired given total and precise collaboration between the American owners and the Allied operators. Known as the 2-key system, this is as watertight as it is possible to make it.

The supposed military function of these nuclear weapons is fourfold. They are to kill the crews, or seriously impede the function of attacking tanks, guns, armoured personnel carriers and missile launchers – particularly nuclear. They are to render inoperable enemy command, control, communications and intelligence gathering systems. They are to destroy or disrupt enemy reinforcements massing deeper in enemy territory. And they are to destroy fixed installations such as airfields, bridges, marshalling yards, ammunition dumps and other military facilities. Obviously there have always been other, sometimes equally effective, ways of coping with all these 'targets'. For the last thirty years, however, nuclear warheads have been seen as having special utility because their potentially enormous explosive yield could effect, by single bombs, shells, missiles or land-mines, what would otherwise need hundreds, if not thousands, of non-nuclear weapons to achieve, and it could not be done 'economically'. To give a concrete example, a squadron of fifteen tanks strung out along half a mile of road could be knocked out by a single nuclear artillery shell. With non-nuclear artillery shells the job could hardly be done at all – many thousands would probably do no more than blow away the aerials and crack the optics of some of the tanks, and crater the roadway ineffectively. It is important to note that the relative ineffectiveness of ordinary shells is due to their inherent lack of accuracy and lack of destructive effect. To these points we return.

The accepted wisdom has been that in North-West Europe, on certain assumptions, the Warsaw Pact could so outnumber NATO in tanks, guns and tactical aircraft, in a major conventional assault, that only by nuclear means could NATO halt the advance. It has, however, equally been recognised that in purely military terms this doctrine of 'deliberate escalation' is highly questionable. For one thing, due to the emotive impact of 'going nuclear', and because of the high likelihood that to do so would cause huge damage to the population and fabric of Western Germany, any such decision would be long delayed and might in the event never be forthcoming. Consequently, from the point of view of military planning, 'worst case' analyses have to assume that so long as a coherent defence can be maintained nuclear release will not be given. Once a coherent defence is no longer sustainable military planners lose interest! The other snag is that if it is assumed that any use of nuclear weapons by NATO would be answered by the Warsaw Pact in kind – as seems overwhelmingly likely – then any military advantage to NATO would be completely cancelled. Self-evidently, the more destructive a war becomes, the more it is likely to favour the big battalions.

But this discussion does not exhaust the supposed military usefulness of a nuclear arsenal to NATO. Two other points in particular are pressed. First, so long as these weapons are available to NATO, Warsaw Pact planners are bound to consider the *possibility* of their being used. This means that from the outset of any campaign they will be compelled to hold their forces in a high state of dispersal. They cannot risk the concentration of force appropriate to the blitzkrieg tactics of the Second World War, since to do so would invite intolerable destruction if NATO did 'go nuclear'. This dispersal makes the task of the defender much more manageable. Second, it is held that the possession of nuclear weapons by NATO, if it does nothing else, is likely to deter the Warsaw Pact from any 'first use' of theirs. Both these points are almost certainly valid, but what is sauce for the goose is sauce for the gander. If the Warsaw Pact is deterred from 'first use' by NATO's capability the reverse is likely to be true. *Any* such use on this argument is self-deterring. If so, the needs of mutual deterrence and of enforcing dispersion could be met by a rough balance of capability at an immeasurably lower level than now pertains – probably a few hundreds, if not tens of warheads on either side, bearing in mind that each single warhead equals one 'Hiroshima'.

Finally it is argued, with still greater cogency, that the existence of nuclear weapons on the Western side, coupled with the doctrine of 'deliberate escalation', is the best guarantee against any kind of conflict breaking out across the inner German border. (It should be a truism, but is not universally recognised, that no one has a greater stake in the maintenance of peace in Europe than the military. American servicemen and women and their families in Western Germany number half a million souls, the British over 100,000.) One cannot, of course, prove a negative: it cannot be demonstrated that the absence of war in Germany since 1953 is due to the possession of nuclear weapons by NATO. The existence of a robust conventional capability and, more significantly still, the political cohesion and self-confidence of the Alliance have been factors of enormous importance. Nevertheless, the fact remains that despite ugly episodes within the Eastern Bloc, the calm along the border has been broken only by the occasional land-mine, automatic weapon or killer-dog directed upon hapless Eastern Europeans seeking to escape. The suggestion that the existence of nuclear weapons in NATO has contributed to this outcome cannot be categori-

cally denied. The paradox is that if it is true this effect of
mutual deterrence is provided above all by the probability
that any use of nuclear weapons, on however small a scale,
would be likely to engulf the whole of Europe by the process
of 'escalation'.

Battlefield nuclear weapons are an important link. Because
of their comparatively short range they are likely to be
overrun early in a fluid retreating battle. To prevent their
being lost before they can be used, and because of their
comparatively low destructive effect, it is these weapons that
are likely to be called for first. However unlikely it may be in
practice that authority for their use would be delegated, this
possibility remains. It is precisely this supposedly greater
usability that gives battlefield nuclear weapons their ambiva-
lent significance. On the one hand, by decreasing the likelihood of any war breaking out they contribute, however
marginally, to raising deterrence. On the other hand, because
they make it more likely that any war which did break out
would become nuclear they contribute, however marginally,
to lowering the nuclear threshold. This Promethean dilemma
has been at the heart of the argument over battlefield nuclear
weapons from the outset. Since the alternatives are incom-
mensurate the argument cannot be rationally resolved.
Meanwhile public concern is justifiably mounting. The pre-
mium to be gained from some escape from the 'first use'
paradox is growing and this has brought into sharper focus
the need to strengthen the non-nuclear capability of the
Alliance.

NATO has already responded to this imperative with some
degree of urgency. During the late 1970s two brigades were
added to the American army in Europe, and heavy equipment was stockpiled for four more reinforcing divisions. In
the late 1970s, the Alliance agreed to aim for real increases in
defence expenditure of 3 per cent a year, and while not all
nations have met this target the general effect has been to
increase significantly the total of defence spending. Also in
the late 1970s, the Alliance agreed to a Long Term Defence
Programme of Improvements, which included measures to

improve readiness, reinforcements, air defence, communications, command and control and electronic warfare. Thus many improvements have been made to NATO's conventional defences. In parallel with these some 1,000 obsolete nuclear artillery shells and bombs were removed in 1980 and not replaced.

The impact of ET is related to new tactical concepts being studied within the Alliance, the main emphasis of which is the attack of enemy forces at some depth behind the front line. If enemy forces could be attacked before they reached the battle zone their momentum would be checked and pressures on the defence relieved. This, as was mentioned earlier, is not a new idea. What is new is the possibility of carrying out by non-nuclear means what has hitherto been 'economically' feasible only by nuclear means; of carrying out by unmanned vehicles what has hitherto needed manned aircraft; and by launching these from dispersed sites rather than from immovable (and therefore vulnerable) concrete runways.

The technical mechanisms involved in ET are mostly well proven and need only to be brought together. Conventional explosives, making use of the 'shaped charge' principle, can forge high-pressure jets of metal effective against armoured vehicles at several hundred feet. They can also be arranged in other conformations to attack runways, aircraft shelters, aircraft taxiing on take-off, or any other specific target.

Second, these mechanisms can be provided in miniature form and dispensed – as bomblets or minelets – in large numbers from a single 'delivery means' (aircraft, missile or shell). Third, developments in far infra-red optical systems and in very high-frequency radar, taken in conjunction with the enormous power of on-board microcomputers, makes it possible to equip individual missiles, shells, or even bomblets, with the ability to detect, identify and home in on individual tanks, guns or other armoured vehicles – every time a coconut! Fourth, these 'submunitions' can be carried and dispensed with high accuracy from almost every form of 'delivery means' known to man. Dispensers for manned

aircraft are already in use. Unguided submunitions for artillery shells, rocket-launchers and surface-to-surface missiles
are also available, and their 'terminally guided' counterparts
cannot be many years away. For deeper penetration likely
delivery vehicles include upgraded surface-to-surface and
surface-to-air missiles; variants of the Trident booster or
Pershing II; or derivatives of the air- and ground-launched
Cruise missiles of the Tomahawk family as suggested in the
quotation at the start of this chapter. Almost any combination is now technically feasible – it is very much harder
to devise combinations with highest tactical and also cost
effectiveness.

Nor would any of this make much sense if it were not that
targets can now be located deep within enemy territory –
notably by the new TR-1 reconnaissance aircraft being deployed to RAF Alconbury, which can transmit target information to ground stations, designate targets and provide
weapon cueing or guidance for ground- or air-launched
weapons. And equally revolutionary developments are impending in the field of command, control and communication
systems, and in automatic navigation. These technologies
can already provide dramatic increases in the effectiveness of
non-nuclear weapons. Using the new American multibar-
relled rocket-launcher now entering service, and a terminally
guided submunition in an advanced state of development, it
is already possible to do as much damage by a single salvo as
could be done hitherto by a single nuclear shell.[2] By combining warheads optimised for the attack of runways, with either
Pershing II or Cruise missiles, it will be possible to neutralise
enemy airfields without use of manned aircraft or nuclear
warheads. These, in outline, are the reasons for General
Rogers' confidence in 'the credible prospect that our conventional defence will succeed'.

Many doubts have been expressed about this concept,
which bears all the hallmarks of the American predilection
for a quick technical 'fix'. This makes it all the more important to winnow out what is of genuine strategic value. As
always, where novel combinations of technology are con-

cerned the most serious uncertainties concern the time and cost of implementation. General Rogers has proposed that the annual rate of real growth of defence budgets be increased to 4 per cent from the existing targets of 3. But even the 3 per cent target is proving unattainable at present.

Equipment budgets are in any case largely bespoken for the next five years. It is not until the late 1980s that any scope is likely to emerge for novel technologies. There will also be industrial complications. European nations will not want to buy American weapons or produce them under licence with no share in the advanced technology. Problems over intellectual property rights, sales, work sharing, research and development levies and American reluctance to share technology with their allies will all prove difficult. But such difficulties have been overcome in the past, and it is a reasonable prediction that within the next ten years much of what is now spoken of as ET will be coming into service with the NATO forces; and into the Warsaw Pact not very much later.

At this stage a different class of questions arises. First, is the arrival of these types of weapon system likely to favour defence any more than existing nuclear systems? The answer, if history is any guide, is: 'Probably not for long!' But this in itself does not matter. The important point is that a balance, no more unstable than that existing at present, will be attainable without the need for tactical recourse to *nuclear* weapons. In military terms the gains will be enormous since almost all the constraints applicable to nuclear weapons – delegation, delay, damage limitation – will have been removed. Collateral and unintentional damage is likely to be far less. Above all, the nuclear threshold itself will have been raised greatly.

Will this in turn lead to greater confidence and stability between East and West? If not, then it were better not to embark upon this course. The answer is that greater confidence and stability could emerge if the ground is prepared accordingly. It will be necessary to convince the NATO Allies, above all the West Germans, that the reduced likelihood of escalation will not in turn lead to a serious erosion of deterrence. A similar struggle took place when the doctrine of 'massive retaliation' was supplanted by the present doctrine of 'flexible response'. The transition should not be unmanageable. More difficult to handle, perhaps, will be the response of the Soviet Union. First signs are not encouraging. In conversations at Edinburgh in September 1983 the immediate reaction of the Russian side was to categorise the proposed conventional 'deep attack' system as highly dangerous and escalatory. But even they cannot have it both ways. If the existing NATO doctrine of 'first use' is as dangerous as they aver, and if the nuclear-armed Cruise and Pershing missiles are so threatening, then it must in logic follow that their substitution by conventional counterparts must be an improvement. There is, of course, an obvious problem in the realm of arms control, of distinguishing the nuclear from the conventional missile by some means of external verification. But this has been tackled in the case of bomber aircraft and should not be insuperable for missiles.

And one further enormous benefit would follow: namely the total removal of *all* nuclear systems from large tracts of Europe. Once the Alliance has moved away from the need for a doctrine of early recourse to nuclear weapons, and once the military tasks now allocated to nuclear rockets, shells and aircraft bombs can be largely if not entirely assumed by non-nuclear weapons, then the way is open for a huge reduction in the number of nuclear warheads required – to enforce dispersion and to deter use of nuclear warheads by the other side. This in turn would mean that the residual nuclear role could be taken on, if not wholly by submarines, then by Cruise missiles (whether air, sea or ground launched) far from the inner German border and by aircraft other than those specifically committed to the tactical battle. It has been announced[3] that over the next six years a further 1,400 to 2,000 redundant battlefield nuclear warheads are to be removed from Western Europe. Under the concept discussed here it should be possible to remove twice that number, or more. This would transform the problem of verification since, as Herbert F. York has observed,[4] 'a nuclear capability consisting of only a few, or even a hundred, nuclear battle-field weapons stored in a few widely separated super-secret locations . . . would not change the military balance significantly'. Above all, the creation of a nuclear-free zone in the centre of Europe, however artificial (in the sense that mobile systems can always be returned, and the point of aim cannot be exported in any case), would nevertheless give a great fillip to the process of confidence-building and arms control. Genuine measures of disarmament might well follow: an outcome profoundly to be hoped for.

_____

1 *Military Technology*, May 1983, p 50.
2 Using, for example, as target the squadron of tanks mentioned earlier in this chapter.
3 *The Times*, October 28th, 1983.
4 *Survival*, September/October 1983, p 231.

For Discussion

1. Do you think that the threat to be the first to use nuclear weapons in a war is immoral?

2. Is there any difference in the threat to use them in retaliation?

3. Ought we to develop new defence policies with a higher dependence on non-nuclear weapons?

Section III

THE GOSPEL AND DETERRENCE

4 THE STRANGE MERCY OF DETERRENCE
The Revd Richard Harries

Everyone now acknowledges that nuclear weapons cannot be disinvented. Scientific knowledge is irreversible. What we have discovered we can never undiscover. Yet it is doubtful if the implications of this have yet sunk in. *The possibility of nuclear war is with us until the end of time*. There will never again be a time on this earth totally free of the fear that nuclear weapons might be used. Suppose a miracle, and nuclear weapons were actually dismantled; still the knowledge of how to make them will be there. If a war broke out the adversaries would rush to their nuclear drawing-boards. For this reason dismantling nuclear weapons *could* actually make nuclear war more, rather than less, likely. For the first power to make a nuclear device would have nothing to deter it from using it.

We have eaten the apple of nuclear knowledge and been expelled from the pre-nuclear world. 'For all our longing to return to the innocence of our lost paradise, there is no going back to Eden.'[1] Nevertheless, it is fundamental to Christian faith that first, nothing happens totally outside God's providence; and secondly, God is ceaselessly at work turning our evil into good. This conviction has expressed itself most powerfully in relation to our redemption by Christ so that as one of the oldest pieces of Christian prose puts it, referring to the sin of Adam: 'O happy fault. O necessary sin of Adam, which gained for us so great a redeemer.' A medieval carol makes the same point in a delightful manner:

Ne had the apple taken been,
The apple taken been,
Ne had never our lady
Abeen heavene queen.

Blessed be the time
That apple taken was,
Therefore we moun singen
Deo Gracias.

The conviction that nothing that happens is outside God's knowledge and permission and that he can twist our wrong-doing to a constructive end, applies to the whole sweep of God's work, not simply to our redemption in Christ. There is a clear example in the way some Christians (e.g. Lutherans) have understood the state. They have pointed out that in the Garden of Eden there was no organised political life and that before the fall, God ruled the world 'with one finger'. The fact that we have states which depend on coercion is a result of the fall. But for the fall coercion would not be necessary. Yet, within the providence of God, even the state is used for good. It is used to keep man's sinfulness within bounds. It is used to limit the harm we can do to one another. So the state is both a result of the fall and a partial remedy for it.

Nuclear weapons are also both a result of, and a partial remedy for, the fall. Nuclear weapons exist because we have eaten that particular apple of knowledge. Yet God does not simply leave us to stew in our own juice. He utilises our sin so that the destructive consequences of it save us as well as threaten us. In particular, he uses the fear of nuclear weapons to deter nuclear powers from going to war with one another. Now, for the first time in human history, it could never be in the interest of a state to go to war against another state possessing nuclear weapons. It would be sheer suicide.

Technology has rushed headlong down human history. Each advance in the destructive power of weapons has been met by a protest; all to no avail. The Church condemned the cross-bow. The Church condemned gunpowder. Yet still we went on inventing ever more destructive weapons. Now God, of his mercy, has turned our instruments of devastation against war itself. Nuclear warfare is not a rational option. However much the two nuclear superpowers huff and puff, both know it and have admitted it. The conviction that a nuclear war between the nuclear powers is as unlikely as anything can be in this world does not rest on a rosy view of human nature. On the contrary, it is based on the certain fact that nations pursue their own interests and that it could never be in the interest of one power to go to war against another power that possessed nuclear weapons. This does not, of course, rule out the possibility of accident or political miscalculation. There is no cause for complacency. Yet the present system of mutual deterrence is far more stable than many people allow, and it seems likely that the present nuclear stalemate will continue for the foreseeable future.

When Joseph's father died, his brothers were frightened that he might take his revenge on them for their ill-treatment of him. But Joseph said to them: 'As for you, you meant evil against me; but God meant it for good, to bring it about that many people should be kept alive, as they are today' (Gen. 50: 20 RSV). Our method of averting war by the threat of mutual annihilation is grotesque and obscene. Yet even in this, God's mercy can be seen. We meant evil against one another but God meant it for good 'to bring it about that many people should be kept alive, as they are today'.

Unrecognised Evils

Those who believe that God has forced nuclear weapons, with their unlimited destructive power, to yield some good – in brief, those like myself who are probably still alive today because of them – nevertheless need to face up to the real evils which their existence either tolerates or promotes. Solzhenitsyn, in his Templeton address given in London on 10th May, 1983, attributed the major problems of the twentieth century to the fact that men have forgotten God:

The same kind of defect, the flaw of consciousness lacking all divine dimension, was manifested after World War II when the West yielded to the satanic temptation of the 'nuclear umbrella'. It was equivalent to saying: Let's cast off worries, let's free the younger generation from their duties and obligations, let's make no effort to defend ourselves, to say nothing of defending others – let's stop our ears to the groans emanating from the East, and let us live instead in the pursuit of happiness. If danger should threaten us, we shall be protected by the nuclear bomb; if not, then let the world go to hell! The pitifully helpless state to which the contemporary West has sunk is in large measure due to this fatal error: the belief that the only issue is that of nuclear weapons, whereas in reality the defence of peace reposes chiefly on stout hearts and steadfast men.

This is a challenging passage both to those who support and those who oppose a policy of nuclear deterrence. It reminds us that under the nuclear umbrella we have had to accept the subjugation of East Germany, Czechoslovakia, Hungary and many other countries. People in these countries have had to live under a system to which they are fundamentally opposed, which has been thrust on them by force of arms, and which is totally contrary to the values in which the West believes. Yet, we have had to accept this situation because we accept, rightly in my view, that any attempt to change the status quo by force would probably lead to a third world war, and that an all-out nuclear war is the worst possible evil we can imagine. We judge that nuclear war would be the worst evil, and therefore we accept lesser evils like the suppression of the Hungarian uprising in 1956 and the freezing of the Prague Spring in 1968. Solzhenitsyn is ambiguous in this passage and does not make it clear whether in addition to 'stout hearts and steadfast men' he believes there should have been armed, conventional attempts to liberate Eastern Europe. If so, I believe he is wrong. Nevertheless, evils have been tolerated, and Solzhenitsyn may be right in suggesting that the West no longer believes in anything enough to fight for it. Instead, we have sheltered under the nuclear umbrella.

The second evil which the nuclear stalemate not only

tolerates but positively promotes is the trade in conventional arms. It is the nature of major powers to expand their power and influence. This is no longer possible in Europe and so the struggle to win friends and influence people goes on overseas. Today it is not so easy as it once was to have bases on foreign shores and therefore the main form in which the power struggle goes on is in the sale or transfer of conventional arms. *In the last decade arms transfers have doubled and over three-quarters of this trade goes to the developing world.*[2] This military hardware is not old surplus, but includes the most sophisticated modern weaponry. A preoccupation with the nuclear issue has blinded the Churches to this problem (which does not admit of simplistic solutions).

A Qualified Acceptance of Deterrence

A policy of nuclear deterrence has enabled the West to avoid a major war and at the same time to witness to its belief in the freedom and self-determination of nations. For this reason the most authoritative Church statements have judged that under present conditions a policy of nuclear deterrence is still morally acceptable. The Pope's statement to the United Nations Special Session on Disarmament in June 1982, which has been highly influential, is nevertheless a very qualified acceptance.

In current conditions 'deterrence' based on balance, certainly not as an end in itself but as a step on the way towards a progressive disarmament, may still be judged morally acceptable.

The General Synod of the Church of England meeting on February 10th, 1983, voted in favour of the following amendment. Synod:

Affirms that it is the duty of HM Government and her allies to maintain adequate forces to guard against nuclear blackmail and to deter potential nuclear and non-nuclear aggressors.

In contrast to the provisional, highly qualified, conditional nature of the Pope's statement, this is a robust defence of the duty of a government to its people. Deterrence is not simply 'morally acceptable', it is seen as a positive duty. It emerged in private discussion and correspondence with the proposer of this amendment, the Bishop of Birmingham, that in an article on its significance I did not properly stress the word 'adequate' in the motion.[3] This is a fair point. Although the word is vague, the Bishop used it to point to a policy of *minimum* deterrence, as opposed to a policy based on a strict parity of weapons systems.

The United States Roman Catholic bishops, in their important pastoral letter, were decisively influenced by the Pope's statement, though they subject deterrence to more detailed examination than he did in his United Nations speech and arrive at an even more conditional acceptance.

In concert with the evaluation provided by Pope John Paul II, we have arrived at a strictly conditional, moral acceptance of deterrence. In this letter we have outlined criteria and recommendations which indicate the meaning of conditional acceptance of deterrence policy. We cannot consider such a policy adequate as a long-term basis for peace.[4]

The Roman Catholic Bishops in Germany take the same view:

This moral toleration of the deterrent depends on the fulfilment of very strict conditions which must be all the more strict, the shorter the time at our disposal becomes.[5]

These statements point to a concept of 'Just Deterrence', analogous to the concept of a Just War, i.e. a concept of deterrence which sets strict limits and conditions to what may be deployed. These criteria would point in the direction of a 'minimal deterrence', i.e. one which rests on the certainty of unacceptable damage rather than one which tries to match weapon system to weapon system.[6]

Why Christians should support deterrence

At the debate of the General Synod, the motion in favour of a unilateral renunciation of nuclear weapons by Britain was defeated by three to one. Similarly in the 1983 General Election, the Labour Party's unilateralist policies were decisively rejected by the electorate. Nevertheless, although the debate against unilateralism was won, it was won on rational and ethical grounds. It has not yet carried *Christian* conviction. Most British people actually think along the lines, 'Of course, if you were a true Christian you would be a pacifist, certainly unilateralist'. They think this, even though they themselves, on rational and ethical grounds, reject both pacifism and unilateralism. The Christian pacifist and the Christian unilateralist are both able to carry conviction because their Christian commitment and their political commitment hang together, the one seems to arise out of the other. The non-pacifist and multilateral points of view, however, are commonly felt to be a kind of Christian sell-out. There is a *Christian* case, however, for affirming the duty of HM Government, or any government, 'to maintain adequate forces to guard against nuclear blackmail and to deter potential nuclear and non-nuclear aggressors.' The Christian case is based on a simple premiss and its implications. The premiss is that until the parousia, the coming again of the Lord in glory, God *wills human life to continue*. The implications of this are twofold. First, God wills human society to continue, for 'mind is a social reality'. Human minds can only exist and develop in relation to other minds. Secondly, he therefore wills the means without which no human society can exist.

Everyone, except anarchists, accepts this in relation to the internal life of the state. We support the police, for example, with their power to apprehend and detain wrongdoers. We know that if we want human life more advanced than that of cave-dwellers to continue, we have to maintain the conditions which make organised political life possible, even though this inevitably involves some use of force.[7] What applies to the state is no less true in the international order. Some people

draw a sharp line between the state, where they accept the
need for some coercion, and the international order, where
they reject it. But there is an unbroken continuum between
the individual state and the states system as a whole. The
radical, tragic difference is that at the present stage of
evolution there is no international authority with the power
to enforce its decisions on a nation determined to reject them.
So if all else fails each nation has to act as advocate, judge and
law enforcement officer in its own cause. Yet this unhappy
situation cannot alter the fundamental principle. So long as
God wills human life to continue, he wills us to maintain the
conditions without which no human life is possible. The
alternative is sheer anarchy. We reject anarchy within the
state. It should be equally decisively rejected in the states
system as a whole. This means that from a Christian as well as
a moral point of view, aggressors must be resisted. Bullies
should not be tolerated whether on a school playground or in
the international order. In resisting them we are co-operating
with God in his work of maintaining the essential pre-
conditions for the development of the human mind.

God has given *us* this responsibility. This means, in the
international order, working for a basic *pax-ordo-iustitia*.
Some people, while agreeing with this in principle, say: 'Only
so far and no further. There are some steps we cannot take,
some things we cannot do – and one of these is to use or
deploy nuclear weapons.' There are two points to be made
about this. First, *The Church and the Bomb* does not, in my
judgment, succeed in its argument that nuclear weapons are
intrinsically immoral in a way that other weapons are not.
Most uses of nuclear weapons would certainly be immoral.
But, in theory, not every use would violate the principles of
discrimination or proportion.[8] Even the US Bishops Pastoral
Letter, which goes as far as it can in condemning possible
uses of nuclear weapons, does not unequivocally condemn
every use. Even apart from arguments over the nature of
intention, that is enough from a moral point of view to allow
for the deployment of nuclear weapons for deterrent purposes. Secondly, those who say, 'Thus far, and no further', are

in danger of handing over the international order to lawless-
ness. They are allowing potential adversaries to think that if
only they raise the stakes high enough they can get what they
want. It is a moral imperative of the highest order that people
should not be allowed to believe this: we do not accept it in
relation to terrorists. Thus when terrorists hijack a civilian
airliner, the international community as a whole accepts that
they must not be allowed to get away with it, even if the
attempt to foil the terrorists results in loss of civilian life.
What the international community accepts in relation to
terrorists is even more important to accept in relation to
states. This is not only a moral imperative. For a Christian it
is co-operating with God in enforcing his law.

Where do we go from here?

Christ's words, 'Blessed are the peacemakers', impinge on us
all. There are many steps on which Christians can unite to
make that peace more of a reality. One of them is to support
steps to make us less dependent on nuclear weapons. Now,
for the first time, as a result of the new precision-guided
weapons it may prove possible over the next decade to have
an adequate conventional capability; that is, the capacity to
stop an enemy advance without having to resort to nuclear
weapons. Those who are anxious to move away from nuclear
weapons need to grasp this nettle – for there is an economic
and political cost to be paid.

Support for a stronger conventional capability is not in any
way to encourage the idea that a conventional war would be
acceptable. A conventional war in Europe, with modern
weapons, would be more devastating than the Second World
War. The point about increasing our conventional strength is
that these weapons could actually be used. Deterrence depends not only on the weaponry available, but no less on the
enemy being convinced that they will be used. Professor
Wolf Graf Von Baudissin, who commanded the West German army after the Second World War and who fought in it
until he was implicated in the plot against Hitler, told me
that the decisive factor in the German invasion of France was

not lack of weapons. The French did possess weapons. What they lacked was the will to resist. The only truly significant factor in the Falklands war was the signal it sent out of our will to resist aggression. It strengthened our whole deterrence strategy. 'The defence of peace reposes chiefly on stout hearts and steadfast men,' said Solzhenitsyn. In almost every situation that one can think of it would be irrational and insane to use nuclear weapons. The same judgment does not apply to the use of conventional weapons. The enemy can conceive of our resisting, and resisting strongly, with conventional weapons. So an adequate conventional capability strengthens deterrence, which is what it is all about. Deterrence is still, and must remain, the name of the game. Strengthening the conventional option does not mean, however, that war is going to be made manageable and acceptable, because the use of any weapons in Europe would be unpredictable. This thought has a desired side-effect. As Professor Lawrence Freedman has put it:

> In practice, a strengthening of conventional forces strengthens pure deterrence, by ensuring that an aggressor cannot predict with confidence the results of a clash of forces in the centre of Europe.[9]

The Churches press us to go down the road of mutual and verifiable nuclear disarmament. How far would it be right to go down that road? I sometimes imagine a fairytale in which President Reagan and Mr Chernenko are walking in the woods together. Every other nuclear power has dismantled its weapons and the two superpowers have scaled theirs down to a minimal deterrence. In the woods, President Reagan and Mr Chernenko agree on procedures of verification and both are willing in principle to take the final step and abolish the last nuclear weapons in their possession. Yet otherwise the world remains unchanged. The same differences of ideology and perspective remain, the same potential for developing new weapons, the same conventional armies, the same possibility of wicked men arising and leading people astray.

Would it be right for them to conclude an agreement? It *may* be right, but it is not obviously right.[10]

---

1 Alan Booth, *Shalom* study pack – available from: 85 Marylebone High Street, London, W1M 3DE.

2 Andrew Pierre, *The Global Politics of Arms Sales*, Princeton, 1982.

3 'Nuclear Weapons: The General Synod Decision in the Light of Day' in *Crucible*, April–June 1983.

4 *The Challenge of Peace: God's Promise and our Response*, CTS/SPCK, 1983, P.V – see also pp 46–57.

5 *Out of Justice, Peace*, Irish Messenger Publications, Dublin, 1983, p 57.

6 See my 'The Morality of Nuclear Deterrence' in: *What Hope in an Armed World?*, ed. Richard Harries, Pickering and Inglis, 1982, p 87.

7 This use of force is not incompatible with the purposes of love. See my 'Power, coercion and morality' in *The Cross and the Bomb*, ed. Francis Bridger, Mowbrays, 1983.

8 I have tried to show this in *Christian*, Vol 7, No 2; and in *The Cambridge Review*, May 1983.

9 *What Hope in an Armed World?*, p 48.

10 See my, 'Conventional Killing or Nuclear Stalemate?' in *Unholy Warfare*, ed. D. Martin and P. Mullen, Blackwells, 1983.

For Discussion

1. 'We have eaten the apple of nuclear knowledge.' Do you think that the idea of deterrence, set out by Richard Harries, helps us to come to terms with the bomb in a responsible Christian manner? (Compare this chapter with Alan Kreider's contribution.)

2. In the light of this chapter, discuss what you think President Reagan and Mr Chernenko should agree as a result of their walk in the woods (page 72).

3. What are the strengths and difficulties of the argument advanced in this chapter?

5 THE GOSPEL NO TO THE BOMB
Dr Alan Kreider

'A large-scale nuclear exchange would be a calamity unprecedented in human history.'[1] So concluded a recent scientific study for the US Congress. But how calamitous would nuclear war be? No one knows. Within the past five years, however, many of the world's scientists have begun to think hard about this question. Their findings are unsettling.[2] Britain, it is clear, would be heavily attacked. And as a result of the attack, British people would fare badly. Agriculture would be severely disrupted, leading to famine and starvation; medical services would collapse, exacerbating the spread of epidemic disease; democratic political institutions would disintegrate. Even organised religion (including the established Church of England) would probably wither; the Government (a Home Office minister recently stated) has 'no plans at present for offering accommodation to ministers of religion of any denomination in headquarters for regional government in war', either as chaplains to those serving there or as pastors to potential survivors outside.[3]

It could be the case, a British Medical Association report speculates, that a few million Britons might survive. But they would not do so as an industrial society – not even as a 'rural civilization of two centuries ago', for the equipment and skills of primitive technology have long since disappeared.[4] It is also possible, however, that all Britons – indeed all inhabitants of the Northern Hemisphere – might eventually die in what leading American scientists have called a 'severe extinction event'.[5] Alerted by the Mount St Helen's volcanic eruption, they have calculated that nuclear explosions would thrust so much debris – both smoke and radioactive dust – into the troposphere that the earth would be darkened. Surface temperatures would plummet to as low as −40° C. In this 'nuclear winter', those who didn't freeze to death would die of thirst: you can't drink frozen water.[6] However we conceive it, nuclear war would be an unimaginable attack upon the *shalom* (the wholeness of life and relationships) of God's created order.

No one, of course, wants to commit such an act of blasphemy against the Creator. Most people, including those who daily make, handle and target the nuclear weapons, probably wish that they had never been invented. But for our generation they are a fact of life; and they cannot be disinvented save by the suicidal act of nuclear devastation that would disinvent most other technological devices as well.

How are we, as British Christians in 1985, going to live with nuclear weapons without their devouring us? The 'orthodox', official approach is that of nuclear deterrence.

1 *Realism.* Human nature was profoundly marred by the fall, so that human relationships have become distorted by the misuse of power. Henceforth, the reconciling love which Jesus taught and incarnated is possible for individual Christians; but it is beyond the reach of groups, whose highest attainment is not love but 'justice'. In international politics, this expresses itself in a 'balance of terror', a 'fragile peace which is all our sinfulness allows'.[7]

2 *Lesser evil.* Threatening to incinerate an opponent is an evil thing to do. But it is not as evil as leaving a nation and its values helpless against an antagonistic nuclear power.

3 *It works!* As the current Defence Secretary, Michael Heseltine, has put it, 'The greatest single reason for maintaining our nuclear deterrent is that for 38 years we have kept the peace.'[8]

4 *There is no alternative.* Michael Heseltine is sure that 'to do anything other than pursue the policies that have guaranteed that peace would be a gamble'.[9] Theologian Richard Harries

agrees: 'Nuclear deterrence is the only form of protection against powers that have nuclear weapons.'[10]

So deterrence, its adherents contend, is working; a rather consumptive peace is being maintained; and, if we keep our heads cool and calculate correctly, we won't have nuclear war. The UK must therefore keep its bomb until multilateral negotiations have persuaded everyone else to get rid of theirs.

Deterrence in Difficulty

There are two difficulties with this 'orthodox' doctrine of deterrence: it isn't working as it is supposed to; and it is morally wrong. Let us examine these difficulties in order.

First, the impending collapse of nuclear deterrence. A decade ago deterrence appeared to be (as the saying goes) 'robust'. Both superpowers had a sufficient number of invulnerable weapons to devastate an opponent even after having absorbed an all-out nuclear attack. All nuclear powers were thus self-deterred by 'Mutually Assured Destruction' (MAD). Furthermore, the international climate was relatively friendly; and between the superpowers there was considerable interchange and an element of genuine trust.

Three developments, however, have been undermining this and leading to a strategic environment which, according to Professor John Erickson of Edinburgh University, is 'becoming rapidly destabilized'.[11] The first of these is the sheer momentum of the arms race itself. Technology has marched on, as research scientists produce new weapons which create new strategic possibilities. So nuclear weapons proliferate, both in number and in sheer dispersal throughout the armed forces of the nuclear powers; and doctrines of 'flexible response' and 'nuclear war-fighting' ensue, which assume that, in a war in Europe, the West would be the first to 'go nuclear'. We have, according to the two strategic analysts, been moving from MAD to NUTS – 'Nuclear Utilisation Target Selection'.[12]

Even more ominously, the former invulnerability of second-strike strategic missiles is now being threatened. In part this is a result of developments in anti-satellite and anti-submarine weapons. Even more it is the product of the increased number and accuracy of new missiles, which have made a pre-emptive first strike seem sufficiently possible to be feared by both superpowers. The Americans speak of their 'window of vulnerability'; the Soviets sense themselves surrounded by a 'comprehensive arc of threat'.[13] Indeed, the Soviets are aware that within eight minutes of their dispatch Pershing II missiles launched from West Germany could be landing with remarkable accuracy (twelve times that of the SS-20s) upon command centres in the heart of the Soviet Union. As a result, they have spoken darkly of moving to a 'launch on warning' policy, in which the decision for a massive nuclear attack upon NATO Powers would be taken by computers. So even though the nuclear powers have got more weapons than they used to have, they are becoming less and less secure.

A second destabilising influence is the worsening relationship between the nuclear powers. 'Soviet-American relations', according to US diplomat and Sovietologist George Kennan, 'are at the lowest point in 30 years.' The problem, Kennan contends, goes beyond the 'anxious competition in the development of new armaments'. It is also a competition in rhetoric, in which British and American statespersons attempt to outdo each other in 'this blind dehumanization of the prospective adversary'.[14] Those whom we view as fundamentally different from ourselves we will someday be willing, with little compunction, to annihilate.

A third development destabilising the strategic environment is nuclear proliferation. The danger of the widespread dissemination of nuclear weapons has long been recognised and was the main motivation for the Non-Proliferation Treaty (NPT) of 1968.[15] In Article II of this treaty, the non-nuclear nations agreed not to acquire nuclear weapons. But in exchange, the non-nuclear nations obtained Article VI, which requires the nuclear powers to limit the 'vertical proliferation' (increase in numbers and sophistication) of

their own nuclear arsenals. This Article the nuclear powers
have ignored. Since the SALT I treaty, the superpowers'
strategic nuclear warheads have climbed from 8,200 to
18,500; and the Trident SLBM system in itself represents an
eight- to fourteen-fold vertical proliferation in the UK's
nuclear capacity.[16] Non-nuclear nations are likely to be
equally loth to keep Article II. Indeed, our arguments for our
bomb give them every excuse to acquire their own nuclear
weapons. Not to have nuclear weapons 'would leave a nation
helpless against antagonistic nuclear powers' (Harries).[17]
Why shouldn't every nation – Argentina, Brazil, Cyprus,
and so on down the national alphabet – reason in like
manner?

An arms race that is out of control – a dehumanisation of
our prospective foes and a virtual certainty of proliferation of
nuclear weapons to unstable regimes – this is a recipe for
conflagration. Michael Heseltine is right: for Britain to shift
away from its 'orthodox' policy of nuclear deterrence would
be a 'gamble'. But he is wrong – tragically wrong – in failing
to point out the size of the gamble (with increasing stakes and
virtually no collateral) that Britain is taking every day by
continuing its current policies. President Reagan summed up
the situation admirably: the world cannot go on for long
without 'some fool or some maniac or some accident trigger-
ing the kind of war that is the end of the line for all of us'.[18]

Christian Perspectives

So nuclear deterrence is not working; it is also, from a
Christian perspective, morally monstrous. Let us consider
the moral issues.

In the first place, by our policy of nuclear deterrence we are
saying that we are willing to 'sacrifice everything for the
truth'.[19] The multilayered cultural legacy of the past, the
generations of the future, the human family of the present –
we are willing to contemplate the destruction of all of these in
a monumental *Götterdämmerung*.

How seriously we take ourselves! How prideful we are to
entertain this act of 'race suicide'![20] Are our perceptions of

truth so sure, and the survival of our nation-states so vital, that we are willing to sacrifice by fire what is not ours but the Lord's – 'the world and those who dwell therein' (Ps 24: 1)? If so, we must consider whether, in a biblical perspective, our values and nations have become idols.[21] For their sake, it appears, we are willing to offer up millions of *victims* (animal sacrifices) in an earth-searing *holocaust* (whole burnt-offering).[22] A recurrent theme in the Old Testament is that men and women worship what/whom they put their ultimate trust in (e.g. Ps 118: 3–11). It is only when we stop and meditate – bringing the weapons and strategies of our day before the Lord in prayer – that we realise that we have become the devotees of a self-authenticating machine that now threatens to consume us.

Second, by our policy of nuclear deterrence we are saying that for political ends we are willing to incinerate the Christian Church in the Soviet Union. Despite persecution which at times has been systematic and often vicious, the light of Christ has continued to shine there. In fact, there are more believers in the Soviet Union than the total number of Britons of any faith. The estimated percentage of active Christians in the Soviet Union is twice as high as it is in the UK, and the Christian community – though under continued pressure – is growing.[23] The witness of Scripture, and the experience of the early Christians, show that Christian life and values can be refined, but not eradicated, by persecution. But through our nuclear arsenals we are threatening to do with fire what the Soviet régime has failed to do with gulags and psychiatric hospitals. In theological terms, we are threatening to mutilate and amputate the world-wide body of Christ in which we, like the Soviet Christians, are members.

Third, by our policy of nuclear deterrence we are declaring what our priorities are. Because of the West's confrontation with the Soviet Union, our attentions and resources are diverted from the real issues which we face as a world community. We overlook the impending exhaustion of the world's non-renewable natural resources, approximately 20 per cent of whose annual yield is being expended on the arms race and 80 to 95 per cent of which we in the First World consume.[24] We ignore the widening gulf of poverty that separates the rich nations and the poor nations and the rich and poor here in Britain, despite the fact that we know that this disparity is a certain source of conflict. The UK military budget, on the other hand, continues to rise. Despite Cabinet infighting, military spending is 19 per cent higher in real terms than it was in 1979, while expenditures on social services falter and grants for overseas aid have fallen to a paltry 0.38 per cent of the British GNP.[25] From the perspective of the vast majority of the world's population, the nuclear arms race appears to be yet another luxury of the rich nations, East and West.[26] In St Matthew's Gospel (25: 31ff) Jesus warned his disciples that the nations would be judged by their treatment of the poor and weak, in whom he in a special way would be present. If the Vatican II *Pastoral Constitution* is correct, as I believe it is, in seeing the arms race as 'an act of aggression against the poor', we can expect a severe judgment.[27]

Fourth, by our policy of nuclear deterrence we are bringing upon ourselves and our children not peace but the steady erosion of *shalom* which fear always engenders.

For many Westerners, the nuclear threat has given us our first real taste of powerlessness. Far-reaching decisions about nuclear policy (e.g. Chevaline, Trident) are taken, not by Parliament, but by small committees of 'experts'. For good reason we feel that there is nothing that we can do. Our children feel similarly helpless. It is not surprising that youths in the nuclear age have found it difficult to form stable ideals or establish long-range relationships. All of us – young and old – experience what Yale University psychiatrist Robert J. Lifton calls 'double-life', in which we fear that nuclear war may break out at any moment, yet we go on living in routinised ways as if everything were normal.[28] 'We looked for peace, but no good came, for a time of healing, but behold, terror' (Jer. 8: 15 RSV).

Fifth, by our policy of nuclear deterrence we are conceding that where the vital interests of our nation appear to be threatened there are *no limits* that we will put upon the use of violence. This is a serious matter, for until very recently Christian thinkers, aware of the inexorable thrust of warfare towards atrocity, have always insisted upon imposing limits on military violence. This was certainly true of the Christian thinkers of the first three centuries, all of whom espoused the non-violence which grows most naturally from the teachings of Jesus.[29] Time and again they repeated Jesus' first ethical teaching in the Gospel of Luke (6: 27 RSV) – 'Love your enemies' – for such love was both a sign of their conversion and a means of achieving the new humanity in which both they and their enemies were being incorporated.

Theologians in the Just War tradition, which has dominated Christian thinking from the fourth century until today, have been similarly concerned to limit the violence of war. The Just War theory, we must remember, was an attempt to restrict warfare, not to justify it.[30] A war could be just if, and only if, three conditions were met.

1 *right intention*; soldiers, even in the thick of the fight, must 'cherish the spirit of a peacemaker'.

2 *just cause*; war is only just if it is a response to a manifest violation of justice.

3 *just means*; the means must be *proportionate* – not wreaking more havoc than was warranted by the original injury. The means must also be *discriminate* – soldiers will be just only if they restrict their killing to other combatants, and do not extend their violence to civilians, women and children. There is a difference, Just War theorists have maintained, between war and massacre. For example, a war which begins in response to a just cause, if waged in an unjust manner, ceases to be a just war, and killing in it becomes murder.

4 *The 'Nuremberg principle'*; if the war is not just, the Christian must refuse involvement, if necessary by disobeying orders and taking the consequences.[31]

It is not difficult to see why nuclear weapons have placed the Just War theory under considerable strain. After all, the bomb that devastated Hiroshima was massively indiscriminate, killing 135,000 people, mostly civilians; and there are today over 50,000 nuclear weapons, with a total explosive power of 12,000,000 Hiroshimas. Some theologians have recognised that the nuclear weapon is inherently indiscriminate; but, since they are convinced that it would be politically irresponsible to abandon the bomb, they have instead abandoned the Just War theory. By doing so, they have left behind any Christian conceptual framework for limiting the violence of war.

Other theologians have tried to maintain both the Just War theory and the bomb. They have done so primarily by means of two arguments. The first admits that nuclear weapons are potentially indiscriminate and disproportionate, but denies that they must necessarily be that. For not all nuclear weapons are designed for counter-city targeting; some are quite small, including nuclear artillery shells and nuclear depth bombs. Intercontinental ballistic missiles, if precisely targeted against military installations, could theoretically achieve a result that is relatively discriminate (and thus, in intention, morally justifiable).

These uses for nuclear weapons might, in theory, be discriminate and proportionate. In practice, however, they are anything but that. The US, for example, in its Single Integrated Operational Plan has 40,000 potential nuclear targets, none of which is 'population *per se*'. But sixty of these non-civilian nuclear targets are in Moscow alone, and many additional ones are (in American military jargon) 'co-located with population centres'.[32]

There is hardly a responsible analyst who believes that nuclear war can be contained. The late Lord Mountbatten in one of his last speeches asserted with some passion, 'As a military man I can see no use for any nuclear weapons which would not end in escalation, with consequences that no one can conceive'.[33]

The second argument by which Christian thinkers have sought to keep both the Just War theory and the bomb is that of the 'just deterrent'. Using nuclear weapons, they concede, would be immorally indiscriminate; but possessing them as a means of keeping the peace by deterring other nuclear powers from using their weapons in battle or blackmail is legitimate. Of course, this means threatening to do something evil (e.g. targeting Moscow with Polaris missiles); but it is less evil than surrendering cherished values as a result of refusing to employ nuclear weapons as a deterrent.

Theologians debate whether it is as immoral to threaten to commit a genocidal act as it is actually to commit it. My inclination is to take Jesus' words very seriously (Matt. 5: 28) when he says that what we think in our hearts is as spiritually significant as what we do. Those who plan for nuclear war have already fought it in their hearts.[34] But even if a 'conditional threat' to commit a monstrous deed were morally tolerable, it would be so only as long as one could be certain that the threat would never need to be carried out. That is the wobbly edge of the deterrentist's position. For a threat to be credible it must be backed up by actual military hardware, competently manned by well-drilled personnel who are ready at all times to carry out orders. The advocates of 'just deterrence' assume that the orders will never come. But they cannot prove their assumptions, and deterrence seems to be running out of time.

Nevertheless, the advocates of nuclear deterrence persist in rushing down this deadly cul-de-sac. They do so because they are convinced that – despite the risks, despite the mounting horror of our predicament – 'there is no alternative'. Like the victims of a cobra, the advocates of nuclear deterrence – and the rest of us with them – are transfixed by the sight of our destroyer. We are immobilised by the power of a strategic doctrine which presents itself as an unchallengeable inevitability. We are trapped. 'The nations', wrote the Psalmist, 'have plunged into a pit of their own making; their own feet are entangled in the net which they hid' (Ps. 9: 15 NEB).

Personal Conversion

Can we break loose? Not *unless* we allow God to work in our lives to open our eyes to possibilities, rooted in his Way, which we have only dimly discerned. We need to see the world anew, to perceive ourselves (and our enemies) from a perspective that is both humbler and more exalted. We need to sense that God does indeed manifest his power in history, but in ways other than overwhelming strength (2 Cor. 12: 9). We need, in short, to experience conversion. And this is happening to an increasing number of people these days: to the evangelist/theologian Michael Green, while meditating on the power-in-weakness of Christ's nativity; to Robert Aldridge, Christian aeronautical engineer, while reflecting on the 'one-dimensional concern' which he shared with the other researchers on the Trident missile project; to Leroy Matthiesen, Roman Catholic Bishop of Amarillo (Texas), while listening to the troubled conscience of a Christian who worked in a local US Department of Energy plant, thereby learning of the presence, in his diocese, of the final assembly plant for US nuclear weapons.[35] The penny drops. People, confronted with truth and with the reality of their own complicity, in repentance begin to engage in lateral thinking. They begin to live in a new way and to think new thoughts.

This repentance is costly. It is affecting, sometimes in a quite profound way, the personal lives and routines of an increasing number of Christians. It is affecting their religious lives. Their prayer takes on new dimensions.[36] Through confessing their sins and fears, the roots of war in their own hearts are withering away.[37] By learning to pray for their rulers and enemies (1 Tim. 2: 2; Matt. 5: 44), and by pleading for *shalom* (Ps. 122: 6), they are discovering new dimensions of intercession. They are discovering that worship is more relevant than they had imagined possible. With Jeremiah they are finding that they must speak out, especially in response to fellow Christians who – as the world crisis deepens – keep saying, '"Shalom, shalom," when there is no shalom' (Jer. 6: 14). This renewal is affecting other areas of their living. Asking themselves whether paying taxes for nuclear weapons is any more justifiable than it was to pay to operate gas chambers in the Nazi holocaust, they are beginning to support the Peace Tax Campaign. In their concern to counteract the dehumanisation of the enemy, they are struggling against considerable odds to visit the Soviet Christians. Some of them are twinning their congregations with others in Eastern Europe. And when facing the reality of jobs that design and produce weapons that will be used in nuclear war, some Christians are in faith entering the wilderness of unemployment. In the nuclear age, these people are discovering that there is a God-kindled 'fire in their bones' (Jer. 20: 9) which requires a deeply personal response.

Policy changes

Renewal is also leading many Christians to go beyond the 'orthodox' theory of deterrence. Their thinking is not uniform, but in its very diversity it is pregnant with possibilities. It has the enabling power of an idea whose time has come.

There are indeed alternatives – a staggering, liberating thought. Some of these alternatives represent only slight modifications of current Western military policy; others are more radical. But almost all of them involve a significant component: a unilateral initiative by the West. In 1979 Pope John Paul II admonished us, 'Make gestures of peace, even audacious ones, to break free from vicious circles.'[38] In a struggle in which both competitors are becoming exhausted and increasingly insecure, the interests of both can be heightened by the stronger party taking the initiative to change the nature of the contest.

Soviet superiority?

The stronger West – how unfamiliar that sounds to Western ears. We are, as Gregory Treverton of the International Institute for Strategic Studies once remarked, so accustomed to hearing of our military inferiority that we have come to believe it.[39] But let us consider the situation from the standpoint of the Soviet leaders. The Soviet leaders are of course aware that, in the SS-20s, they have got vastly more land-based Long-Range Theatre Nuclear Weapons (LRTNWs) in Europe than NATO has. But they also know that this gives them scant advantage, for in overall nuclear capacity (number and accuracy of warheads) the Soviet Union is inferior to the West.[40] And they recognise that the idea of a nuclear war limited to Europe, which is the only event in which it makes sense to view the LRTNWs as a category distinct from the total arsenals of the superpowers, is 'dangerous nonsense'.[41] Indeed, they are probably more worried by the newly-deployed Pershing II and Cruise missiles than the West is by the SS-20s, for the pinpoint accuracy of the Western missiles threatens their command centres with first-strike destruction. Even the immense strength of their conventional forces can hardly be reassuring to the Soviet leaders. For they know that their five million troops face NATO and Chinese forces each of which has equal numerical strength;[42] their advantage in battletanks is blunted by NATO's preponderance in technologically sophisticated anti-tank guided weapons;[43] and their navy, for all its new cruisers and aircraft-carriers, lags far behind the US in its capacity to project power around the globe. To cap it all, the Soviet leaders realise that although they are crippling their economy by their vast military expenditures they are falling behind the richer West. US Secretary of Defense, Caspar Weinberger, is right: 'The combined resources of the United States and its allies dwarf those of the Soviet orbit.'[44]

Western response

In this setting the Western nations must take the initiative. They must act, not because they have any illusions about the benign nature of the Soviet government, but because they know that it is an illusion to think that there will be anything but war if they do not act. Despite their keen sense that they are threatened by the Soviet Union, they must act in the confidence that they are strong enough to take the necessary initiatives. And Christians must be there, thinking imaginatively about alternatives and, where possible, using their political leverage, to help the governments to slow – and then reverse – the arms build-up step by step.

By speaking of 'step by step' action I am recognising that the world cannot vault to our ideal destination from our present position of peril in one heroic leap. Many pacifist

Christians would prefer to have our populace well-trained in the methods of non-violent civilian-based defence;[45] and many Just War adherents would ideally choose a non-nuclear, non-threatening form of defensive deterrence.[46] But both of these goals are distant ones, and we must be realistic about the long hard road to military conversion. We must never lose sight of the policies which would be consistent with our Christian convictions; and as individual disciples and as communities of faith we must live resolutely in light of these. But equally it is our Christian duty to think practically about middle axioms, policies which we right now could ask a government, in view of its values and commitments, to adopt.

Principles to practical politics

A middle axiom is not an ideal policy; it is not fully in keeping with Christian principles. But by the same token it is not a moral monstrosity. The middle axiom is somewhere in between.[47] It takes a step of courage informed by principle to get from where we now are to a first middle axiom. And when we have got there, far from relaxing our efforts we must propose a further middle axiom and provide the arguments and political pressure necessary to move towards it.

By this process, Just War adherents can realistically expect Britain, in the not-too-distant future, to arrive at a non-nuclear military posture which is in keeping with their convictions. Pacifist Christians, on the other hand, are unlikely ever to see a major country defended by non-violent methods. Nevertheless, from middle axiom to middle axiom, they strive towards these. In a fallen world, pacifists realise they will probably never achieve a policy that is as non-violent and just as biblical teachings would require. But they also sense a prophetic Christian political calling to try to secure policies that are *more peaceable and more just* – and more like the Kingdom of God – than governments think are possible.

Unilateral steps

The military posture of both East and West, Just War adherents and pacifists agree, is morally indefensible;

threatening to kill millions (and possibly billions) of innocent people cannot be justified. The military situation is also extremely dangerous, as humanity careers towards the precipice of world war. Somehow we have got to extricate ourselves from this desperate situation.

Christians in Europe and North America who adhere to the Just War and to pacifism are beginning to point to a different way. 'Since in the present climate of mistrust it is too hard to achieve progress by multilateral negotiations alone', they are saying, 'the West must proceed unilaterally.' There is no hope for peace until one side – *our* side – gives a lead and takes steps towards disarmament.

We are sufficiently strong that we can afford to make concessions that will be major enough to convince the Soviet leaders of our peaceful intentions – they in time will feel safe enough to respond, because a de-escalation of the arms race is also in their interests. That would break the log-jam of negotiations which have been stymied by the insistence on 'negotiating from (superior) strength', and in time it may lead to genuinely productive talks. Professor Keith Ward is correct: 'There is immense scope for some unilateral steps.'[48] And these are more likely to lead to multilateral disarmament than are our present rigid policies.

In their search for middle axioms, Christians should be urging NATO countries immediately to take three unilateral steps:

1 De-escalation of righteous rhetoric: when our leaders repeatedly say that our enemies, unlike ourselves, are embodiments of evil, there is no hope of progress at the negotiating table. Such statements are also theologically objectionable. Original sin, the Christian Church has maintained, is universal and does not begin at the East German border.

2 'Freeze': a unilateral halt by NATO of the testing, production and deployment of new nuclear weapons systems. In order to slacken the pace of the race and allow trust to develop, we must stop where we are. Our military forces are incredibly powerful already.

3 Nuclear-free corridor in Central Europe: a unilateral withdrawal by NATO of all nuclear weapons from the East–West border area.[49] These 'battlefield' nuclear weapons are particularly dangerous. They threaten the civilian population as much as the troops; there is real pressure to use them early since they may be threatened with capture in the early days of a war; and if they are used, they will almost inevitably be the fuse that would ignite all-out nuclear war.

These would be a good start. They would, of course, put pressure on the NATO forces to defend their territory by conventional means. Many NATO generals are convinced that this could be done. For several years their commander-in-chief, General Bernard Rogers, has been arguing for such a strategy.[50] But his plans for conventional war are still threatening; his enemies can easily perceive his 'AirLand' battle doctrine, which calls for 'Deep Attack' upon their forces, as aggressive.[51] It would be far better, as the Just Defence movement has argued, for NATO to develop a military posture which would be specifically defensive and non-provocative. The microchip technology in which the West excels has given a substantial advantage to 'smart', defensive weapons. These are also often cheaper.[52] If NATO were to be imaginative and to adopt a policy that was structurally non-aggressive as well as non-nuclear, we might not only have a reduction in the level of tension in Central Europe; we might even save some money.

None of these three unilateral initiatives by the NATO nations goes far enough to achieve a military posture that all Christians – pacifists as well as Just War adherents – can be content with. But they are middle axioms, steps in the right direction. And they are of immense practical value in themselves. They are likely to induce a climate of trust in which the Soviet Union would feel itself secure enough to respond to Western initiatives.

British Initiatives

Britain, as a major and potentially influential member of NATO, might take the lead in these alliance-wide initiatives.

As *The Church and the Bomb* rightly argued, Britain can do something even while remaining in NATO. While retaining potent conventional forces, she can unilaterally renounce her 'independent' nuclear weapons; and she can deny British bases to the nuclear forces of her erratic American ally.

This is not because I have any hope of an atomic immunity for Britain. In a nuclear war, Britain – even without US nuclear bases – would probably be hit by both bombs and fall-out, although less devastatingly than if US bases were still present. It is rather for reasons both moral and political. I need not belabour the moral reasons. And politically, I am intrigued by the possibility that, within the framework of the NATO alliance which would retain an incredible armoury of nuclear weapons, a rejection of nuclear weapons by Britain might play an important role in a process of global disarmament. And the time is short.

So Britain should act in the present crisis, not for self-protection, but because this may be our last chance to be *great* in the biblical sense of the term – as the servant of others (Luke 22: 26). Surely unilateral nuclear disarmament would not be what the new Archbishop of York fears, 'further evidence of a British decline'.[53] It would rather be a sign of the realism and settled courage of national maturity.

By disarming nuclearly, we should be joining a new club – the club of 152 sovereign states who do not have the bomb. We should have joined them by taking an action which ended the vertical proliferation of our own weapons, thereby keeping our side of the Non-Proliferation Treaty. And we should be sending a message of unique authority to the non-nuclear nations who at this moment are being tempted to disregard their side of the Treaty: 'The bomb is evil. It has not led to our security, and it will not lead to yours, either.' With the other non-nuclear nations we should be facing the possibility of blackmail by a nuclear power. But with them we should be recognising that the possible scenarios for nuclear blackmail are far more distant, and morally far more acceptable, than the pressingly urgent scenarios for nuclear holocaust with which our Civil Defence planners are working. The fruits of this nuclear disarmament are impossible to predict; the calculus of risk is imponderable. But in a modest way we should have done something instead of simply being co-operative as we are herded along to our generation's equivalent of the gas chambers. And who knows? We may have helped to turn the tide.

Turning the Tide

History records dozens of major crises in which the tide turns. Old ideas give way to new. Old orthodoxies, which at first had seemed to fit the facts and had then been maintained through mental and moral laziness, gradually come to appear questionable. After a period of restlessness, in which no concept seems to be appropriate, a new idea emerges to which thoughtful people – with increasing unanimity – say 'yes'!

Conversion is now taking place among an increasing number of Christians in relation to war. No longer is the statement by the pagan Roman General Vegetius, which has been repeated ad infinitum by Christian Europeans, credible: 'If you wish for peace, prepare for war.' Lord Mountbatten was unerring in his instinct that this statement was 'absolute nuclear nonsense'.[54] And it is the nuclear bomb – 50,000 plus of them – which is concentrating the mind of many other people on the matter. In the light of the prospect of nuclear war, the US Roman Catholic bishops have discerned a truth that has been present all along and is only now becoming apparent: 'If you wish for peace, defend life.'[55]

We are faced with a choice, between 'life and death, blessing and curse' (Deut 30: 19 RSV). The choice is not an easy one. The old paths are well-worn and sanctioned by tradition; yet if we continue on them, we sense that the Lord will 'deliver us into the hand of our iniquities' (Isa. 64: 7 RSV). In our crisis time, God is calling us into the insecurity of blazing new trails and of giving political expression to the 'justice, peace and joy' (Rom. 14: 18 NEB) that are the hallmarks of his Kingdom.

1 US Congress, Office of Technology Assessment, *The Effects of Nuclear War* (Washington DC, Government Printing Office, 1979), p 3.

2 For recent examples see S. Openshaw, P. Steadman and O. Greene, *Doomsday: Britain after Nuclear Attack* (Basil Blackwell, 1983); British Medical Association's Board of Science and Education, *The Medical Effects of Nuclear War* (John Wiley & Sons, 1983).

3 Douglas Hurd, MP, to Sir Hugh Rossi, MP, 28 July 1983, communicated to me by Sir Hugh Rossi, 3 August 1983.

4 BMA, *The Medical Effects of Nuclear War*, p 123.

5 P. R. Ehrlich and 19 other scientists, 'Long-Term Biological Consequences of Nuclear War', *Science*, 23 December 1983, p 1299.

6 R. P. Turco et al., 'Nuclear Winter: Global Consequences of Multiple Nuclear Explosions', *Science*, 23 December 1983, pp 1282–92.

7 Most Revd and Rt Hon Graham Leonard, Bishop of London, in *The Church and the Bomb: The General Synod Debate, February 1983* (CIO Publishing, 1983), p 9.

8 *The Times*, 4 May 1983, p 4.

9 Ibid.

10 Revd Richard Harries, 'The Morality of Nuclear Deterrence', in idem, ed. *What Hope in an Armed World?* (Pickering & Inglis, 1982), p 99.

11 Professor John Erickson, Radio 3 broadcast, text personally communicated to me by Professor Erickson, 5 October 1983.

12 Spurgeon M. Keeny Jr and Wolfgang K. H. Panofsky, 'MAD vs NUTS: The Mutual Hostage Relationship of the Superpowers', *Foreign Affairs*, Vol 60 (Winter 1981/1982), pp 287–304.

13 International Institute for Strategic Studies, *Strategic Survey 1980/1981* (IISS, 1981), p 14; Professor Erickson, broadcast talk.

14 George F. Kennan, *The Nuclear Delusion: Soviet-American Relations in the Atomic Age* (New York, Pantheon Books, 1982), pp 187 and 141.

15 For the Non-Proliferation Treaty see T. N. Dupuy and G. M. Hammerman, eds, *A Documentary History of Arms Control and Disarmament* (New York, R. R. Bowker, 1973), pp 561–4.

16 *World Armaments and Disarmament, SIPRI Yearbook 1981* (Taylor & Francis, 1981), p 275; *SIPRI Yearbook 1983*, pp 48–9.

17 Revd Richard Harries, 'The Morality of Nuclear Deterrence', p 105.

18 *The Times*, 17 May 1983, p 1.

19 Ulrich Simon, 'A Lamb to the Slaughter', in Francis Bridger, ed., *The Cross and the Bomb* (A. R. Mowbray & Co, 1983), p 107.
20 Emil Brunner, *The Divine Imperative: A Study in Christian Ethics* (Lutterworth Press 1937), p 471.
21 Bob Goudzwaard, *Idols of Our time* (Inter-Variety Press, 1984).
22 Dale Aukerman, *Darkening Valley: A Biblical Perspective on Nuclear War* (New York, Seabury Press, 1981), p 56.
23 David B. Barrett, *World Christian Encyclopedia* (Nairobi, OUP,) 1982), p 689; Walter Sawatsky, *Soviet Evangelicals Since World War II* (Kitchener, Ontario, Herald Press, 1981), p 14; Nationwide Initiative in Evangelism, *Prospects for the Eighties: from a Census of the Churches in 1979* (The Bible Society, 1980), p 15.
24 Oral communication, October 1983, from John Mitchel, Director, World Development Movement.
25 *The Times*, 7 July 1984, p 4.
26 Andrew Kirk, 'An Uncomfortable Message', *Grassroots*, September/October 1983, p 10.
27 US Catholic Bishops' Pastoral Letter, *The Challenge of Peace: God's Promise and Our Response* (The Catholic Truth Society/ SPCK, 1983), p iii.
28 Robert Jay Lifton, 'In a Dark Time . . .', in Ruth Adams and Susan Cullen, eds, *The Final Epidemic: Physicians and Scientists on Nuclear War* (Chicago, Educational Foundation for Nuclear Science, 1981), p 9.
29 Jean-Michel Hornus, *It is Not Lawful for Me to Fight: Early Christian Attitudes toward War, Violence and the State*, revised edition (Scottdale, Pa, Herald Press, 1980).
30 For a recent summary of the Just War criteria, see *The Challenge of Peace*, pp 24–32.
31 'If a subject is convinced of the injustice of a war, he ought not to serve in it, even on the command of the prince' (Francisco de Vitoria, *De Iure Belli*, in Albert Marrin, ed., *War and the Christian Conscience* (Henry Regnery Co, Chicago, 1971), p 89.
32 Desmond Ball, *Targeting for Strategic Deterrence*, Adelphi Paper 185 (IISS, 1984), pp 32–3, 40; Sir Solly Zuckerman, *Nuclear Illusions* (Collins, 1982), p 56.
33 Lord Mountbatten, 'The Final Abyss?', speech on the occasion of the award of the Louise Weiss Foundation Prize to the Stockholm International Peace Research Institute (SIPRI), Strasbourg, 11 May 1979, reprinted in *Apocalypse Now?* (Spokesman Books, 1980), p 11.
34 R. A. Markus, 'Conscience and Deterrence', in Walter Stein,

ed., *Nuclear Weapons and Christian Conscience* (Merlin Press, 1961/1981), pp 65–88.

35 Michael Green, 'Preface' to R. J. Sider and R. K. Taylor, *Nuclear Holocaust and Christian Hope* (Hodder & Stoughton, 1983), p 13; Robert C. Aldridge, *First Strike!* (Pluto Press, 1983), p 16; Leroy T. Matthiesen, 'I Didn't know the Gun was Loaded', in R. J. Sider and D. J. Brubaker, eds, *Preaching on Peace* (Fortress Press, 1982), pp 30–1.

36 Richard Foster, 'Prayer and Holy Obedience: Discipleship in a War-Racked World', *Grassroots*, January/February 1984, pp 14–17; March/April 1984, pp 18–19, 27.

37 Thomas Merton, *New Seeds of Contemplation* (New York, New Directions, 1961), p 122; Kenneth Leech, *True Prayer: An Introduction to Christian Spirituality* (Sheldon Press, 1980), ch 3.

38 Cited by Mgr Bruce Kent, 'A Christian Unilateralism from a Christian Background', in Geoffrey Goodwin, ed., *Ethics and Nuclear Deterrence* (Croom Helm, 1982), p 63.

39 Gregory Treverton, *Nuclear Weapons in Europe*, Adelphi Paper 168 (IISS 1981), p 14.

40 *SIPRI Yearbook 1983*, ch 3; Paul Rogers, *Guide to Nuclear Weapons* (School of Peace Studies, University of Bradford, 1984).

41 BBC Radio 4 programme on Cruise missiles, 10 October 1983.

42 *The Military Balance 1981–1982* (IISS 1981), pp 73, 124. The 1983 edition of *The Military Balance* (pp 138–9) suddenly adds 1,500,000 troops of uncertain provenance to the total of the Soviet armed forces; cf. Andrew Kelly, *Not by Numbers Alone: Assessing the Military Balance* (School of Peace Studies, University of Bradford, 1984), p 50.

43 E. Dinter and P. Griffith, *Not Over by Christmas: NATO's Central Front in World War III* (Anthony Bird/Hippocreyne, 1983), p 44.

44 *The Times*, 10 March 1983, p 8.

45 R. Sider and R. K. Taylor, *Nuclear Holocaust and Christian Hope* (Hodder & Stoughton, 1983), ch 13–15.

46 F. Barnaby and S. Windass, *Non-provocative Defence* (Just Defence, 1983, available from Just Defence, The Rookery, Adderbury, Banbury, Oxon, OX17 3NA).

47 J. H. Yoder, *The Christian Witness to the State* (Faith & Life Press, 1964), pp 72–3.

48 K. Ward, 'Christians and Cruise', *Church Times*, 10 February 1984, p 11.

49 Palme Commission, *Common Security: A Programme for Disarmament* (Pan Books, 1982).
50 General Bernard W. Rogers, 'The Atlantic Alliance: Prescriptions for a Difficult Decade', *Foreign Affairs*, Summer 1982, pp 1145–56.
51 B. D. Sutton et al., 'Deep Attack Concepts and the Defence of Central Europe', *Survival*, Vol 36 (March/April 1984), pp 50–70.
52 P. F. Walker, 'Precision-guided Weapons', *Scientific American*, August 1981, pp 21–9.
53 Dr J. S. Habgood, *The Church and the Bomb: The General Synod Debate*, p 60.
54 Mountbatten, 'The Final Abyss?', p 13.
55 *The Challenge of Peace*, p 81.

For Discussion

1. Is it ever right to threaten the use of nuclear weapons? (Check the point of view of this chapter against the view put by Richard Harries).

2. What do you think are the practical consequences of repentance for our life-style in the age of the bomb?

3. Must Christians be unilateralists?

Section IV

THEMES FROM CHRISTIAN FAITH

6 THE BIBLE ON WISDOM AND PEACE
The Revd Canon Douglas A. Rhymes

Schumacher has said, 'We are now far too clever to be able to survive without wisdom. Knowledge without wisdom can lead to disaster'.[1] My dictionary definition of wisdom is 'the ability to make the right use of knowledge'. An observer in the Middle Ages is reported to have said of the future, 'Under the new methods science will increase but wisdom will decrease.' Etienne Gilson, in summarising the philosophy of St Augustine, paraphrases the distinction Augustine makes between science and wisdom thus:

> The object of wisdom is such that, by reason of its intelligibility alone no evil use can be made of it; the object of science is such that it is in constant danger of falling into the clutches of cupidity, owing to its very materiality. Hence the double designation we may give to science according as it is subservient to appetite, as it is whenever it chooses itself as its end, or is subservient to wisdom, as it is whenever directed towards the sovereign good.[2]

It is because there is a profound difference between the attitude of the old sciences and the new that our world is now in danger of allowing science and technology to separate themselves from wisdom and simply see the world and nature as a quarry to be exploited, irrespective of the use being put to its results.

Wisdom in the Biblical Tradition
It is then from these standpoints of the difference between

knowledge and wisdom that we need to understand the
Biblical view of wisdom in the Wisdom literature of the Old
Testament and the Apocrypha. This may enable us to know
how to use wisdom in making decisions regarding our attitudes to peace and to the retention and use of nuclear
weapons.

a) *Wisdom in the Bible is always linked with the health and
creativity of God's creation.*

This is based upon the knowledge of the interdependence of
all things and the unity of God's creation. Wisdom is always
allied with life and creation not with death and destruction:

> Do not court death by the error of your ways,
> nor invite destruction through your own actions.
> Death was not God's doing,
> he takes no pleasure in the extinction of the living.
> To be – for this he created all;
> the world's created things have health in them
> in them no fatal poison can be found and Hades holds no
>   power on earth.

> But the godless call with deed and word for Death
> counting him friend, they wear themselves out for him
> with him they make a pact and are fit to be his partners
> (Wisd. 1: 12–end JB).

The results of unwisdom are arrogance, annihilation and
deserts:

> We have left no path of lawlessness or ruin unexplored
> we have crossed deserts where there was no track
> (Wisd. 5: 7 JB).

Wisdom understands the interconnectedness and unity of
God's creation. To have wisdom is to be seeing and acting in
the world with that divine intelligence which sees the
interdependence of all things. Wisdom was beside God

before the creation of the world because wisdom is the spirit of life itself against the negative spirit of destruction and death:

> We are indeed in his hand, we ourselves and our words,
> With all our understanding, too, and technical knowledge.
> It was he who gave me understanding of all that is
> who taught me the structure of the world and the
> properties of the elements
> the beginning, end and middle of the times.

> all that is hidden I have come to know
> instructed by wisdom and designed them all
> (Wisd. 7: 16–21 JB).

Contrary to the Biblical view of wisdom human progress has been a purely rational and intellectual affair, a one-sided evolution which has given us enough nuclear weapons to destroy the entire world and enough dangerous nuclear plants to produce massive quantities of radioactive waste that threaten to extinguish life on the planet. There has been an inbalance in our culture – what the Chinese call the *yang* side of ourselves – the active, rational, competitive, scientific has taken precedence over the *yin* – the contemplative, intuitive wisdom, religion, co-operation. We have reversed the Biblical order: 'She [i.e. wisdom] is a breath of the power of God hence nothing can find a way into her', and as a result the whole world has become impure. The true joy of man is to be with God in maintaining the order and unity of his world:

> I was by his side, a master craftsman,
> delighting him day after day
> ever at play in his presence
> at play everywhere in his world
> delighting to be with the sons of men
> (Prov. 8: 30–1 JB).

b) Wisdom is indispensable to rulers.
It is constantly maintained in all the Wisdom literature
that the fate of a country is dependent on the wisdom of its
rulers:

> By me monarchs rule and princes issue just laws
> by me rulers govern and the great impose justice on the
>   world
> (Prov. 8: 15–16 JB).

> an uneducated king will be the ruin of his people
> a city owes its prosperity to the intelligence of its leading
>   men
> The government of the earth is in the hands of the Lord
> he sets the right man over it at the right time
> (Ecclus. 10: 3–4 JB).

It is made clear that wisdom in rulers is a restraining
influence over natural feelings of anger:

> scoffers set cities in ferments but wise men moderate anger
> (Prov. 29: 8 JB).

> by whipping up anger you produce strife (Prov. 30: 33 JB)

> The fool comes out with his angry feelings
> but the wise man subdues and restrains them
> (Prov. 29: 11 JB).
> (See also Eccles. 4: 13).

Many a time in the Wisdom literature the author is
insistent that wisdom is greater than power as many a ruler
understands it:

> the gentle words of the wise are heard above the shouts of a
> king of fools. Better wisdom than warlike weapons, but
> one mistake undoes a great deal of good (Eccles. 9: 17–18
> JB).

A ruler must beware of hasty judgments which will cause bloodshed and he must also be able to be objective about his own self-interests:

> a sudden quarrel kindles fire, a hasty dispute leads to bloodshed. Blow on a spark and up it flares, spit on it and out it goes: both are the effects of your mouth (Ecclus. 28: 11–13 JB).
> (See also Ecclus. 37: 7–10, 16).

I think these quotations are sufficient to show that in the eyes of the Wisdom literature the wise ruler is one who is in close alliance with the designs of God, works for the unity of God's creation, exercises a restraining influence upon his words and actions, is not motivated by self-interest and is always concerned to promote peace rather than strife. It is constantly emphasised how important is the wisdom of the ruler to the fate of his kingdom and people and never would it have been considered that decisions could be made by machines without the human wisdom which is closely aligned to the mind of God.

c) *Wisdom is not necessarily associated with power as the world understands it.*

The Wisdom literature is, on the whole, averse to the idea that strength lies in force and in strength of arms – that which appears to be less powerful may have a power greater than armies:

> There are four creatures little on the earth
> though wisest of the wise,
> the ant, a race with no strength
> yet in the summer they make sure of their food;
> the rick rabbits, a race with no defences
> yet they make their home in the rocks
> the locusts, these have no king
> and yet they all march in good order;
> the lizard which you can catch in your hand
> yet it frequents the palaces of kings
> (Prov. 30: 24–8 JB)

'There was a small town with only a few inhabitants; a mighty king marched against it, laid siege to it and built siege works around it. But a poverty stricken sage confronted him and by his wisdom saved the town . . . wisdom is better than strength.' In everything in life there are two forces at battle with each other – a creative force and a destructive one. Those who recognise wisdom are those who ally themselves with the creative forces of the world, who see the meaning of the world as life not death, those who recognise in creation the unity of the whole world and its interdependence, those who seek to apply to their leadership of the world that alliance with unity, moderation and peace, and those who recognise that power lies often in principle and strength of right rather than in force and armed strength. Moreover, since wisdom is associated with divine intelligence the care of the world must always lie in the brains of men who are in harmony with the divine intelligence. Never can a blind mechanical science take away the human power of decision and choice.

It is in the light of the understanding of the biblical view of wisdom that one can now begin to apply these discernments of wisdom to the present situation of the maintenance of peace and the control of nuclear weapons. I shall confine myself to the implications of these basic three principles of a wisdom ethic.

1. MAN NOW POSSESSES SOURCES OF CREATIVE POWER WHICH COULD ENABLE HIM TO WORK CONSTRUCTIVELY WITH GOD'S CREATION BUT ONLY IF HIS INTELLIGENCE IS GUIDED BY THAT SENSE OF CREATIVE AND UNITIVE PURPOSE.

Man has 'been given unprecedented creative and transformative power for building the world of the future'[3]. The new resources of nuclear energy may harness solar power for useful purposes, fertilise deserts, unlock sub-nuclear energy and develop novel forms of life and even control heredity and sex. There is a new source of power available to man which is not just a re-using and re-developing of present forces but an unlocking of the key to what was considered a new and inviolable part of the universe. But all this can turn to ruin if man does not work *with* God in the use of this power. He can work against God in two ways. Either he can feel himself helpless before the new powers which are being opened up for his use because he only sees their destructive capacity; or he can attempt to unite the new powers with no longer usable ideologies or political ideas so that he will fail to realise how much responsibility for creative and transformative endeavour and policies such power demands.

The possession and building up of nuclear weapons is contrary to the whole idea of man as working *with* God in creation because it leads either to a sense of helplessness before inevitable doomsday or simply to that naked threat of power by which one nation tries to be God as against another – superpower ranged against superpower without any sense of accountability to the rest of the universe – or to feeble attempts to work old concepts of national sovereignty which are an avoidance of the responsibilities which nuclear science forces upon us. Each of these in turn can now be considered more fully.

First, there is no doubt that an increasing number of people do feel themselves helpless before the so-called forces of ultimate annihilation. Humphrey, in the Bronowski Memorial Lecture of 1981, said, 'when human beings believe themselves helpless, helpless they become,' quoting George Kennan, former US Ambassador to Russia who said, 'We have gone on piling weapon upon weapon, missile upon missile . . . like the victims of some sort of hypnotism, like men in a dream, like lemmings heading for the sea.' But Humphrey replies to Kennan, 'When a lemming runs to destruction it runs on its own four feet. It is as individuals that we can and might apply the brakes and as individuals that we can and do fail. The bomb is not an uncontrollable automaton and we are not uncontrolling people.' In other

words he is rightly urging us to make our voice felt along with
God for a world of the future in which we do not face,
hypnotised, a terror of inevitable war. Peace is both possible
and certain provided we work consistently for it, grasp what
it means and what it requires of us towards those who govern
us and provided we never rest in our opposition to a world
gripped by terror and by massive overkill of weapons. We
forget sometimes our own power which can be used when
millions of people want something badly enough. The massive protests at present going on throughout Europe are proof
of this.

Second, at the present moment two powers seem consistently to act as though they were Gods – both America and
Russia seem to regard the world as made to bend to their
will – each not only fearing the other but continuing to build
massive strength beyond all possibility of need against each
other and against the rest of the world. Both superpowers
seem to expect us to regard all the areas within their hemisphere as theirs by right, to intervene and pressurise and even
at times to invade. So Russia acts towards Poland and
Afghanistan, so America acts towards Central and South
America. But wisdom decrees that God has only given to the
peoples of the world the right to inhabit the world for the
benefit of all men – there is no concept in God's philosophy
of wisdom as the rights of a superpower – it is doubtful if the
divine intelligence would even favour the idea of a superpower – empires often found short shrift in God's plans in
the Old Testament!

Third, we have to challenge the very concept of national
sovereignty in the present situation. We are living in a world
where the increasing unity and interdependence of the world
is daily, by science, being brought home to us. By degrees
what is being revealed is that the natural species of man does
not exist by supplanting but by intertwining. Here Teilhard
de Chardin claims that whereas other species of nature
tended to diverge and spread apart, with man the branches of
his species followed an entirely different course. 'Instead of
separating and detaching themselves from one another they

turn inwards and presently intertwine so that by degrees races, peoples, nations merge together to form a sort of uni-conscious super-organism.'[4] But what is happening is that nations are still living in a world where divisiveness prevails politically and economically. This is hopelessly out-of-date in a world which has discovered nuclear energy. It is as if we are trying to contain old concepts of a nationhood in a world which has shown us by God's wisdom in every field of life and science its interdependence. We are keeping within national barriers what has far outpassed such barriers and left them behind long ago. We should not consider it sensible to see England divided again into Wessex, Mercia or Northumbria and Kent, but we are willing to see a world which is as united by nature as is England divided by arbitrariness into the wills of the USSR, US, UK, etc.

But have the statesmen of the world seen this obvious result of the ordering of God's creation in their ordering of the world? When we find Reagan and Chernenko shouting at each other across the barriers of overkill nuclear weapons; when we find wars in the Middle East over small-scale religious and national differences; when we find divisiveness over race, aid to combat poverty, the United Nations reveal-ing not the unity but the disunity of nations; then one begins to wonder why a world united by modern science still behaves as though it were in the Middle Ages. The nation-state has clearly to disappear as an instrument of power inappropriate to the forms and scientific advances of modern society. Teilhard de Chardin is optimistic: 'Mankind is not only capable of living in peace but by its very structure cannot fail eventually to achieve peace. Peace shows us two com-plementary faces: first a steep slope only to be climbed by constant effort in the face of many setbacks: and ultimately the point of balance to which the whole system must inevi-tably come. Peace therefore is *certain*: it is only a matter of time'.[5] There is not, however, much evidence of this con-sciousness of the unity of God's world which is both a lesson of the wisdom ethic and the basis for the certainty of peace. Such consciousness would lead the superpowers to bend *all* their energies to finding means of arms reduction rather than the somewhat lukewarm efforts which seem at present to govern the talks in Geneva. Is the wisdom then of our rulers commensurate to the responsibilities which confront them? That is the next question to which I am led.

2. THE WISDOM OF OUR RULERS.

The wisdom ethic lays great stress on the necessity for wisdom in our rulers. This is, of course, reasonably obvious when such immense technologies capable of world destruction are at stake. Schilling says, speaking of the new nuclear powers given to mankind:

> What is needed is a radically different pattern of human attitudes and commitments and basic to this a further development of human consciousness especially in the direction of increased altruism and a keener sense of responsibility for the common good . . . a radically transformed ethos and mythos of technology, of its proper function in society, of the kind of ideals and ethical standards by which it should be evaluated and governed; ways by which it can contribute to the qualitative improvement of life and to the achievement of peace and tranquillity in their richest sense. Peace conceived of as 'shalom', a rich freight of futurist meanings and ideals which may be summarised by the term 'peace' conceived as the 'harmony of harmonies', this is the peace on earth to men of goodwill of the Christmas story.[6]

In other words what is needed of our rulers now is not to be bending their energies to ways of balancing equality of nuclear weapons, but to seeing how the quantity of unused human energy which is growing at a disturbing rate, owing to unemployment and a certain collapse in moral restraints, may be channelled from the chaos of armed conflict, or violence within society, to those vast new fields of conquest which science has now disclosed to us for human advancement. By that the old battles of war will appear trivial and outmoded – the nuclear age is not meant to be one of destruction but one of unlimited research for human benefit.

But have we the leaders equal to this task? The Chernenkos, Reagans and Thatchers of this world do not show any awareness that this is the main function of nuclear research today – rather do they see the new weapons as allied to the old struggles of a pre-nuclear age and this is the horrifying prospect. Moreover, there is also a new danger – that because human skill is unequal to the task of controlling nuclear war response, the machine is to take over – the final abdication of human wisdom! Has mechanical computerised technology taken over the final decisions for the unleashing of war? It would seem so from recent writings. In an article in *The Listener* on the new American plan for antiballistic missiles by which missiles aimed at America could be destroyed in space before they reached their target, the writer says, 'for the new ABM system to work it will have to be run by machines' – such is the limited time in which these nuclear laser systems would have to work, siting, attacking and destroying within 250 seconds. The human brain is quite incapable of acting so promptly and making such decisions. The USA has already started to produce super-computers which will be planned to carry out all the operations of warfare and the only part the human being will play will be to turn the machine on and off. This is the final abdication of wisdom.

Yet President Reagan is foolish enough to speak of this as a 'vision of the future which offers hope' on the principle presumably that if the USA is rendered invulnerable to attack then the other side will accept for ever this superiority. But has there ever been an arms race in which the other side has not discovered a means of countering, or perhaps, if driven to panic, launches a pre-emptive first strike before the final invulnerability is put into place? The writer of the article in *The Listener* does not share Reagan's optimism: 'In turning to the scientists for the tools to create strategic security the President has formally sanctioned a new arms race which even his most sincere and respected critics believe must end in

Armageddon.' Moreover, quite apart from the fallibilities of
any machine, if the machine is now able to control the
destinies of nations, where is the possibility of that moment
of reflection which the old 'hot-line' gave? 'Today we still
have a few precious moments to think, reason and cool down
and judge against the destruction of the Northern Hemisphere. In President Reagan's brave new world of strategic
defence these minutes will have been replaced by milli-
seconds; and human judgment and compassion by the cir-
cuits on a silicon chip. How can that prospect enhance
international security?' (*The Listener*, 9 September, 1983).
What would the author of the Book of Wisdom say to such an
abdication of man's mind and control over creation?

3. WISDOM LIES IN POWERLESSNESS OR IN THE POWER OF RISKS FOR PEACE.

Both in the teaching of the Wisdom ethic in the Old Testament and in that of the Gospels and Epistles there is the
constant questioning of material power as a means by which
evil is overcome. When there is quoted 'better dead than red'
as sometimes a justification of even nuclear war against the
Soviet Union it is well to remember that non-resistance was
preached as a Christian message when life was under a foreign
conqueror – the Roman Empire. During the writing of the
Wisdom books the Jews were under Greek domination. The
Gospel of Matthew was written for Jewish-Christians shortly
after the fall of Jerusalem – addressed therefore to a defeated
nation. The Epistles were written to groups of people of
different nationalities, but *all ruled* by Rome. The idea of the
strength of the powerless, the *active* non-retaliation of Matthew and the Epistles is not the passivity of one who feels
powerless but the power of non-violence as an *alternative*. It is
the powerlessness of a Gandhi or a Martin Luther King. It is
summed up in the words of Paul: 'For he is himself our peace.
Gentiles and Jews, he has made the two one and . . . has
broken down the enmity . . . so as to create out of the two a

single new humanity in himself, thereby making peace' (Ep. 2: 14–16 NEB). It is a peace and a power which are born out of the hope and power of God.

This kind of power enables us to realise that our present nuclear barriers are born out of fear and insecurity. The Christian sees in the nuclear arms race not a sign of strength but a sign of weakness – the weakness of those who are afraid. He will seek to urge upon his government not deterrents as a means of peace but coming to terms with the ways by which the insecurities of our opponents can be understood and met. Schillebeeckz defends unilateral disarmament as a risk that should be undertaken by Christians:

> Can the vicious circle of the nuclear arms race be broken in any way other than by the 'virtuous' circle of steps towards unilateral nuclear disarmament? This risky trust in unilateral disarmament would appear to be the only concrete possibility for anyone who really believes that Jesus is the Lord of history . . . Christians should risk taking steps towards unilateral nuclear disarmament and Church leaders should have the courage to point the way of this evangelically 'risky trust' as one that believers ought to follow. It is better for us to be martyrs because we refuse to help to prepare for a possible nuclear war than for us to be victims of such a war because we fail to oppose it actively.[7]

Is not the wisdom represented here stronger than the voice of the well-armed? We are always hearing that it would be too great a risk for us to lead the way in unilateral disarmament, but how do we know that our present policies are not a greater risk? Only the future will show which way is true wisdom and at the present moment the risks of escalation and proliferation of nuclear weapons look to many people to be the greater danger. For example, are the policies of the Soviet bloc a reflection of naked aggression or of fear and insecurity of borders? Is the Soviet bloc not also caught up, as the rest of the world, with a spiral of nuclear escalation which is threatening national bankruptcy and crippling her economy?

If the policies are the result of fear would not those fears be lessened if at least one of the lesser nuclear powers showed some evidence of willingness to take a lead in the reduction of weapons?

So much of the struggle between the superpowers is viewed mistakenly as a struggle in ideology between capitalism and communism. Viewed objectively it is in fact, as it always has been, a struggle between rival empires, each fearful of the security of its borders. Under the Czars, the eighteenth century saw the partitions of Poland, the nineteenth century saw three Afghan wars. America has always wanted a 'friendly' Central and Latin America and been prepared to intervene, as we have recently seen, when that security appears to have been threatened. The Soviet Union and China, both communist countries, have nevertheless been at variance because, in reality, they are two rival powers competing, as empires always have, for the security of their borders. Until recently the mutually common ideology of European powers did not prevent them going to war. Biblical wisdom saw the true nature of the conflict in the story of the strong man armed and the stronger who destroys his arms – safety is always threatened by power (Luke 11: 21–2).

Biblical wisdom also speaks of perfect love casting out fear. Why do we so easily dismiss this when it comes to relationships between nations (for, after all, the term 'nations' simply means a small group of human beings in control as against another group of human beings in control). In an article on Gandhi in the September 1983 issue of *Theology*, the author distinguishes two principles: the one – *ahimsa* – not only refraining from violence but reaching out in love to the other; the other – *satyagrapha* (truth force) – the seeking out of what is right in the face of oppression, and a determination to hold fast to the right path come what may. The oppressor is either then forced to intensify his oppression or to acknowledge the wrongness of his stance – if 100 per cent of a people refuse to accept the government of an oppressor, how could he govern? All governments demand some degree of consensus – has *total* passive non-resistance ever been tried? The author of this article concludes with these words,

> I think it is significant that Gandhi appeared on the scene at the threshold of a new era in human affairs; at a time when the decision of a few can literally destroy the human race. We all live under the threat of imminent death; not only from the nuclear weapons that spike this earth, but from the nameless weaponry that as likely as not even now orbits our globe and waits secretly in the chemical arsenals of the so-called advanced nations of the world. It is a moot question whether *ahimsa* or *satyagrapha* can show a way to banish the universal death-threat. But applied to the myriad experiences and events of our individual lives they can lift each one of us personally above this threat's debasing hold.

In that last sentence lies the true wisdom of what we so often preach – the power of love. But even the Church seems very unwilling to trust the power of love when it comes to conflict between nations. Most Christians, like the rest of the world, believe in material, military or economic power. That is why it is often futile and hypocritical to wax indignant against the communists – we are as much materialists as they! Tolstoy, the great Russian pacifist, demanded that people who believe in God should live and act in a different way from those who do not – what hurt him was that Christians behaved exactly in their human affairs as though there were no God. Do we behave as if our protection lies not in God but in nuclear weapons? Was the resolution in the bomb debate more than a cautious middle-of-the-road compromise on nuclear weapons? Are the truly wise the Gandhis, the Luther Kings, the Bishop Tutus of this world, who have a positive view of peace and resistance to evil but who do not see nuclear arsenals as part of that positive view? We live in a world of risks, but the wisdom ethic would see the greatest risk as living in a world *divorced* in its doings from

the creative and life-giving unity with God and his creation
mediated through the wisdom and will to peace of its rulers
and all its peoples.

———————————

1 Schumacher, E., *Guide for the Perplexed* (Cape, 1977) p 66.
2 Gilson, Etienne, *The Christian Philosophy of St Augustine*.
3 Schilling, *The New Consciousness in Science and Religion*, p 262.
4 de Chardin, Teilhard, *The Future of Man* (Fontana, 1968).
5 Ibid., p 152.
6 Schilling, op. cit., pp 265–6.
7 Schillebeeckz, *Concilium: Church and Peace*, p 80.

For Discussion

1. In what ways can the biblical tradition of wisdom help us to make
practical decisions today?

2. In what ways do you consider we are being 'unwise' in our
attitudes towards peacemaking today?

3. Suggest practical endings for the following sentence: 'In the
nuclear age wise rulers should . . .' Justify your ideas in the light of
what you have learnt about biblical wisdom.

7 THE GOSPEL, THE BOMB AND PEACE
The Rt Revd Mark Santer

Christians have always had a bad conscience about fighting in wars. Until early in the fourth century there was a strong tradition that Christians ought not to serve as soldiers – or, if they did, only under conditions that were virtually impossible to fulfil. Those who insisted that soldiering was incompatible with Christianity did so on two grounds. The first was the precept and example of Christ: the Christian must not take life. The second was that it was impossible to serve in the Roman army without becoming involved in idolatry. This was because corporate reverence for the gods and for the statues of the emperors was integral to military discipline. How could you be a soldier without saluting the flag?

Thus, early in the third century, Hippolytus of Rome listed various occupations which disqualified those who practised them from admission to the catechumenate. They included pimps, prostitutes, actors, charioteers and pagan priests. He continued:

> A subordinate soldier is not to kill anyone. If he is ordered to do so, he is not to execute the order, nor is he to take the military oath. If he refuses these conditions, he must be rejected. Anyone who has the power of the sword, or a city magistrate who wears the purple, must either resign or be rejected. Any catechumens or believers who want to become soldiers must be rejected, because they have despised God.[1]

It is, of course, one thing to have principles and another to keep them. It is clear that in fact there were plenty of

Christians in the armies of imperial Rome. St Alban, Britain's first martyr, was one of them. But even when upholding the principle that soldiering was an inadmissible occupation for a believer, Christians still recognised that authority had to be exercised in the world, and that such authority was inescapably coercive. This is the position of St Paul, and it is followed elsewhere in the New Testament (Romans 13: 1–5; 1 Peter 2: 13–14).

Christians could maintain this position, namely of themselves abstaining from the exercise of coercive force while nevertheless acknowledging the need for its exercise within the providence of God, for only as long as they were excluded, or excluded themselves, from positions of public authority. From the beginning of the fourth century, when the emperor Constantine recognised the God of the Christians as the true God, the situation was radically transformed. Public authority was no longer a disagreeably messy but necessary business performed by *other* people, while Christians kept their hands and their consciences clean. From this point onwards Christians found themselves having to take responsibility for the exercise of authority – an authority which included the use of coercive force. This involved not only the maintenance of law, peace and order within the Roman empire, but also defence against external threats.

One must not suppose that the Church immediately abdicated all its standards, or that its bishops gave up on all pastoral discipline of Christians who found themselves exercising coercive authority. Even emperors were subjected to excommunication and penance if they were judged to have committed or permitted acts of inhuman brutality. As late as the battle of Hastings in the middle of the eleventh century Norman bishops imposed a penance of one year for each man killed by the victorious army of William of Normandy. The fact that, in the Middle Ages, such penances could be commuted for money, or be undertaken vicariously, does not detract from the continuing belief that a baptised Christian could not take another man's life, even in service of his prince, without imperilling his own salvation. If one killed, one had to pay for it; if not immediately, then in the hereafter.[2]

But was the Church right to allow a Christian ruler to use coercive force at all? Some Christians – those who take a rigorously pacifist line – would dispute this. Pacifists say (if I understand them rightly) that Christian discipleship excludes every use of violence. They say that it is always counter-productive and that it degrades and dishonours not only its victims but also those who use it.

The argument has much force that it is of vital importance that it should be heard. Nevertheless, the mainstream Christian tradition has not accepted it. But if one is not an absolute pacifist, and if one accepts that force may have to be used in the defence of order and justice, what boundaries is one to set to the use of violence? What are the criteria, if any, for the proper exercise of coercive force? One can find a foundation in the very words of Jesus on which the pacifist builds his argument. 'You have learned that our forefathers were told: "Do not commit murder; anyone who commits murder will be brought to judgement." But what I tell you is this: Anyone who nurses anger against his brother will be brought to judgement' (Matt. 5: 21–2 NEB). In other words, Jesus identifies the spirit of murder as the spirit of destructiveness. The one who will be brought to judgment is anyone who wants his brother or sister put out of the way, anyone who makes of the diminution or annihilation of his brother the price of his own survival. Behind the words of Jesus there lies the story of Cain and Abel: the murderer is anyone who washes his hands of responsibility for the life and health of his brother or his sister. By this teaching Jesus does not deny or contradict the teaching, deeply embedded in the Bible, that it is the task of the ruler to defend the poor and the needy, by force if need be.

Once we recognise that power has to be exercised in the world, we are faced with the task of helping people to exercise it responsibly. That is what Christian moralists and theologians have tried to do, as far as the military use of force is concerned, by developing the doctrine of the Just War. This doctrine attempts to determine both the circumstances in which it may be right to go to war and also the manner in which war may legitimately be conducted. The doctrine of the Just War is expounded with admirable clarity in *The Church and the Bomb*; as in the Pastoral Letter of the United States Roman Catholic Bishops on War and Peace in the Nuclear Age.[3] The points which are of immediate importance for any discussion of nuclear weapons are these:

(*a*) Assuming that the cause for resorting to war is just, there must be a reasonable hope of success, i.e. a reasonable hope of righting the wrong which is held to have justified resort to armed conflict.

(*b*) 'The evil and damage which the war entails must be judged to be proportionate to the injury it is designed to avert or the injustice which occasions it.'[4]

(*c*) 'A good end does not justify all and any means.'[5] From this follow both the principle of non-combatant immunity (i.e. the principle that non-combatants must not be intentionally injured by armed force) and the principle of proportionality (i.e. 'methods of war must not result in disproportionate harm for any of the populations engaged in war or for third parties').[6]

The authors of *The Church and the Bomb* concluded that the character of nuclear weapons is such that their use can in no case satisfy the criteria of the Just War doctrine. In other words, there is no case in which their use could be (or, indeed, has been) morally acceptable. They concluded, further, that the conditional threat to use them is also morally unacceptable. They also point to the provisions of international law. These also enshrine the principles of non-combatant immunity and of proportion, and specifically outlaw the use of particular weapons. These protocols and conventions antedate the invention of nuclear weapons. Nevertheless, it must be noted that in 1961 the General Assembly of the United Nations resolved that the use of nuclear weapons would be 'contrary to the spirit, letter and aims of the United Nations . . . to the rules of international law . . . [and] to the laws of humanity' and would be a 'crime against humanity and civilization'.[7] It is in the light of these international conventions and declarations and of the principle established at the Nuremberg tribunal after the Second World War that a plea of superior orders is no defence against a charge of law-breaking, that a group of officers in the Dutch army have announced that they will refuse to obey any orders connected with nuclear weapons.

Why is the *use* of nuclear weapons morally unacceptable? Basically, because the destruction they would unleash would be out of all proportion to any conceivable cause or purpose. Even a so-called 'limited' nuclear war would be horrific in its effects, and it is generally agreed that, once nuclear weapons were used, escalation would rapidly ensue. Even if it were thought acceptable to devastate the civilian population and the natural environment of one's opponents (a position I do not accept), one would end up with the devastation of one's own population and territory also. The injunction not to injure third parties takes on a terrible new dimension when those involved are not only those living now, but also their descendants – to say nothing of the innocent suffering of animals.

The Archbishop of Canterbury took this position in a lecture at Chatham House in 1983. According to the press, he said that 'a nuclear conflict could never be defended as a just war . . . It would be inherently unjust because innocent civilians would make up the vast majority of those who died'.[8] Similarly, the American Roman Catholic Bishops have asserted that 'under no circumstances may nuclear weapons or other instruments of mass slaughter be used for the purpose of destroying population centres or other predominantly civilian targets.' They went on to express grave scepticism about the possibility of 'limited nuclear war'.[9]

Next, what about the ethics not of use but of *deterrence*? If one concludes that the use of nuclear arms is morally unacceptable, does it follow that it is morally unacceptable to threaten to use them? The paradox of the argument for the use of nuclear weapons as a deterrent is brought out when the authors of *The Church and the Bomb* write: 'The ethics of deterrence are the ethics of threatening to do something which one believes would be immoral, which one intends to do only in circumstances which will not arise because of the conditional threat'.[10] As they put it elsewhere, the paradoxes involved in the theory of deterrence 'may be distilled into one fundamental form, round which the whole debate ultimately revolves: If the deterrent is to work, you have to convince an enemy that you are willing to use it; but if you have to use it, it has failed'.[11] To this one may add that a government can persuade an enemy of its willingness to use the nuclear deterrent only if it also succeeds in persuading its own population that it is willing and ready to use it. When that stage has been reached, surely one may conclude that a government is indeed willing and ready to use such weapons.

Not only is it immoral to threaten an action which you know to be immoral. It is also extremely foolish to threaten an action unless you are prepared to execute it. If politicians decide to use nuclear weapons, they are making an immoral decision. If they decide only to threaten to use them, they are making a dangerously foolish decision. This in such people is in itself morally culpable.

It is well known that not all churchmen accept the judgment of *The Church and the Bomb* that the use of nuclear weapons as a deterrent is morally unacceptable. The Bishop of London, for instance, has said that this judgment

elevates the question of the possession or use of nuclear weapons to one in which a moral prescription is made which admits of no qualifications. In so doing, it removes the necessity to consider the moral demands made by many other issues, such as those of the preservation of liberty, truth and human dignity. It is, I believe, not consistent with the moral nature of man to proclaim one principle of such moral rigidity that these other fundamental moral issues become secondary. Nor do I believe that for a Christian who believes that man is made for eternal communion with the living God who is just and holy can the principle of survival take precedence over all other moral claims.[12]

How do we respond to this? First, I agree that, for the Christian, the principle of survival cannot take precedence over all other moral claims. But that, in my judgment, is not the principle at stake. The principle at stake is that there are some things so appalling that you neither do them nor threaten to do them to your fellow human beings (to say nothing of the rest of creation) even if they do them or threaten to do them to you. We refuse to do them for the very reason adduced by Dr Leonard, namely that we are made for eternal communion with the living, just and holy God, and therefore have to face a judgment for our actions.

Second, although I agree with Dr Leonard that the principle of survival cannot take precedence over all other moral claims, I also agree with what he said in the House of Lords debate on abortion in the autumn of 1982: 'I believe that the right of the innocent to life admits of very few exceptions indeed.' Surely this principle must apply not only to the life of an unborn child but also to the waging of war. This principle, that of the inviolability of innocent human life, is precisely one of the principles which the doctrine of the Just War attempts to protect. It is significant that the American bishops have made this same connection between abortion and the use of weapons of mass destruction. 'Nothing', they say, 'can justify direct attack on innocent human life in or out of warfare'.[13]

Third, far from ignoring those claims of liberty and human dignity of which Dr Leonard rightly speaks, the case of *The Church and the Bomb* is that the use of nuclear weapons would be self-defeating, because they would destroy the conditions in which human beings could enjoy that liberty and dignity which it is wished to preserve. The conditions which would follow the actual use of nuclear weapons would not in fact permit much more than survival, and even that only for some people.

Moving the argument from use to deterrence, the operation of the strange moral law whereby the possession of such weapons rots and undermines the very qualities of life they are supposed to defend can be observed. Far from preserving liberty and human dignity, there are governments in both East and West which are in varying degrees paranoid about security and which isolate and suppress dissent. Our own government, by proclaiming that work for national security is incompatible with membership of a trades union, on the grounds that this necessarily involves a potential conflict of loyalties, has raised an acute question for the Christian conscience. For no Christian can give a loyalty to the state so absolute and unconditional as to rule out the possibility of tension with other, and possibly competing, loyalties. On our television screens we see that dulling of the conscience which has occurred when those who are trained to press buttons deny all human responsibility for the eventual consequence of their actions – 'I am only doing a job'. Yet to deny responsibility is to deny one's own humanity. Part of the corruption of morals is the corruption of language of which George Orwell wrote – as when President Reagan spoke of the MX missile as the 'peace missile'.

Other aspects of official policy should bother us. First, there is the extent to which it feeds on fantasy. There is a quality of self-dramatisation (angels of light versus angels of darkness) which is acutely disquieting. By painting the enemy as demons anything can be justified, even a final orgy of self-destruction.

Second, some attitudes to Eastern Europe betray a fundamental despair about humanity which is in conflict with Christian faith. Soviet rule is terrible: there can be no doubt of that. Nevertheless, it has shown that it is incapable of suppressing human dignity; incapable, too, of suppressing Christianity. It is in fact possible to live in Eastern Europe and to live and die with dignity. The message of the Gospel is that God will indeed redeem his people, even if they have to wait. Reliance on nuclear weapons is tantamount to despair that anything can change except for the worse. It is a denial of the providence of God, it is a form of practical atheism. Furthermore, we have a duty to distinguish the peoples of Eastern Europe, many of them devout Christians and not a few of them persecuted for the faith we have in common, from those who rule over them. Governments have always become anxious when common humanity and common faith have asserted themselves against their ideologies – as was seen in the trenches of Flanders on Christmas Day, 1914. What kind of a liberty shall we give to the peoples of Eastern Europe if, to save them from their bondage, we destroy them in the process? And how shall we live with our own liberty if, supposing we ourselves survive the process, it is bought at the price of their destruction? And how shall we survive the judgment of God?

Third, let us not be confounded by slogans about unilateralism and multilateralism. The real division is not between unilateralists and multilateralists, but between those who are not prepared to wage nuclear war and those who are willing to do it. No so-called unilateralist is opposed to multilateralism, whereas some of those who have recently discovered that they are multilateralists seem to spend more energy on denouncing and abusing those they call unilateralists than in trying to get rid of the threat of nuclear war. That is where we need to concentrate our efforts: on creating the kind of mutual confidence which will allow the superpowers to reach some workable and verifiable agreements. If the unilateral renunciation of the British nuclear element will both contribute to this and help to discourage further proliferation (which is the unilateralism advocated by *The Church and the Bomb*) we ought to do it.

Fourth, there is a direct and inverse relation between the experience and understanding of war and a willingness to undertake it. The people of central Europe have experienced war and do not want it again. That explains the peace movements of West and East Germany, compared with the cheerful readiness of Californian politicians to raise the stakes. For the same reason professional soldiers are often much more humane and discerning than politicians. They know what they are talking about. There are some striking words at the end of Field Marshal Lord Carver's book, *A Policy for Peace* – a book which concludes by arguing for the maintenance of an overall nuclear deterrent, but which mercilessly exposes the folly of any concepts of limited nuclear war, and which leaves the independent British deterrent in tatters:

> There is truth in the maxim of Vegetius: 'Let him who desires peace, prepare for war', but Liddell Hart was right to add that it was above all important that he who desired peace should *understand* war. Such understanding involves an intellectual effort which, unfortunately, few military men, and even fewer politicians, are prepared to make.[14]

Christians know that peace can be built only on a foundation of justice. This in turn must be based on the recognition of our common humanity.[15] Christians also know that true peace can never be bought at other people's expense. We have before us the teaching and example of a Lord who has shown us the only way in which true peace can be had – by paying the price of it himself: 'When he was reviled, he did not revile in return; when he suffered, he did not threaten; but he trusted to him who judges justly . . . By his wounds you have been healed' (1 Pet. 2: 23–4 RSV). Christians know themselves called to share in Christ's ministry of reconciliation; as the Father sent his Son, so the Son sends us as bearers of his peace (2 Cor. 5: 18; John 20: 21). That means that we are called to share in the cost of peacemaking, for there is always a price to be paid. Part of the price is repentance.

---

1 Hippolytus, *Apostolic Tradition* 16.
2 See Southern, R. W., *Western Society and the Church in the Middle Ages* (London, 1970) p 226.

3 *The Challenge of Peace: God's Promise and Our Response* (CTS/SPCK, 1983).

4 *The Church and The Bomb*, p 85.

5 Ibid., p 86.

6 Ibid., p 88f.

7 Quoted in *The Church and the Bomb*, p 80.

8 *The Guardian*, January 26th, 1983.

9 *The Challenge of Peace*, pp 42, 45f.

10 *The Church and The Bomb*, p 98.

11 Ibid., p 153.

12 Leonard, Graham, 'The Morality of Nuclear Deterrence', in *Unholy Warfare*, David Martin and Peter Mullen (Blackwell, 1983) p 187f.

13 *The Challenge of Peace*, p 81.

14 Carver, Michael, *A Policy for Peace* (London, 1982) p 113f.

15 See *The Challenge of Peace*, p 67.

For Discussion

1. Is violence ever justified?

2. Can a Christian be a soldier in an army which may resort to using nuclear weapons?

3. What do you consider to be the cost of peacemaking?

8 THE CHRISTIAN HOPE AND THE BOMB
The Most Revd and Rt Hon Lord Blanch of Bishopthorpe

I began my speech in the bomb debate by saying 'This debate is about the end of the world and about how we may best prevent it or delay it.' The remark provoked a curious subdued ripple of laughter around the assembly hall. At least one reporter in the gallery, who spoke to my lay chaplain afterwards, was extremely puzzled by the reaction. After all, the end of the world was no laughing matter; we were engaged in a discussion about the possible annihilation of the human race. So why did people laugh? I suppose it was because of the sense of incongruity which the remark created. After all, it was rather absurd for the Church to be proposing measures for the prevention or the delay of the end of the world. It is this incongruity which lies at the heart of the Christian hope.

There is nothing new about the fear of universal disaster. The ancient world was haunted by it; astrologers and their customers waited uneasily for that particular conjunction in the heavens which would spell the end of all things. The collapse of the Roman Empire provoked a similar fear that the end of all things was at hand. The Black Death created an atmosphere of deadly fear which, as Barbara Tuchman suggests in her book *The Distant Mirror*,[1] contributed more to the dissolution of society than the plague itself. It is no accident that throughout the Christian era events of this kind invariably produced apocalyptic movements within the Church which were eager to proclaim the end of the world and the coming of the Son of Man – no accident because this is the mental climate which dominates the New Testament.

Against the background of the fear of universal disaster which haunted the ancient world, the Christians stood for a certain kind of hope which is reflected in every tradition of the New Testament. There are the so-called little apocalypses of the synoptic gospels, which you may read in Matthew 24, Mark 13 and Luke 21. There are innumerable references to the Second Coming in the Pauline Epistles, notably in 1 Thessalonians 5 and 2 Thessalonians 2. Then there is the lavish, not to say extravagant, imagery of the revelation of St John the Divine which has never ceased to trouble some and excite others.

It would be easy enough to dismiss all this as the product of a passing enthusiasm. But it is not possible to exclude this element from the teaching of our Lord Himself when it raises its head in parable after parable which are reckoned by most scholars to be original utterances of our Lord. St Paul himself was obviously uneasy with some of the excesses created by this belief among his early converts. He was concerned to lower the temperature, but he never suggested that the faith in the Second Coming of Christ was not part of the authentic Christian tradition. In the minds of these early Christians the Second Coming of Christ was to be associated with some kind of universal disaster –

In those days, after that tribulation the sun shall be darkened and the moon shall not give her light and the stars shall be falling from heaven and the powers that are in the heavens shall be shaken. And then shall they see the Son of Man, coming in clouds with great power and glory (Mark 13, 24–6).

In that same chapter St Mark associates that universal disaster with the particular disaster that in his view would destroy Jerusalem.

When you see the abomination of desolation, standing where he ought not to (let him that readeth understand), then let them that are in Judaea flee unto the mountains.

And let him that is on the house-top not go down nor enter
in to take anything out of his house. And let him that is in
the field not return back to take his cloak (Mark 13,
14–16).

It is not surprising, therefore, that this fervent hope for the
coming of the Son of Man should reach its climax in the siege
and destruction of Jerusalem in the year AD 70. In the Hebrew
mind, Jewish or Christian, such an untold disaster must
herald the end of all things. But the world went on as before,
the Son of Man did not appear, and developing Christian
theology as reflected in the New Testament and in the early
fathers, had to come to terms with this historical dissociation.
St Paul's later letters suggest a different view of the end,
without qualifying his belief in it. St John's Gospel provides,
as it were, alternative sources of hope for those upon whom
the end had not come.

The Church itself is a monument to a disappointed
expectation, with its powerful structures, its long historical
presence, its great buildings, its worldly resources, its claims
and counter-claims to permanence and authority. In the same
series of sessions in which the Church and the Bomb debate
took place, the General Synod of the Church of England was
planning busily for the future, although one might have
supposed from the tone of the debate that there might be no
future. If, therefore, we cannot share in all its fervour this
early Christian hope which dominates the pages of the New
Testament, what hope is there in the face of universal
disaster? As one theologian has humorously put it – 'If
you are standing on the station waiting for a train and you
observe that grass is growing up between the rails, you
may be excused for wondering whether the train still
runs.'

The note of universal disaster and the accompanying
judgment of God is not so prominent in the Old Testament
symphony as it is in the New. But the Old Testament has its
own 'apocalypse' in the book of Daniel, from which the
apocalypse in the New Testament borrows heavily. The

prophet Joel has something to say about 'the valley of decision' when 'the sun and the moon are darkened and the stars withdraw their shining' (Joel 3: 14-15 RSV). The prophet Zechariah envisages the day when God

> will gather all the nations against Jerusalem to battle, and the city shall be taken and the houses plundered and the women ravished; half of the city shall go into exile, but the rest of the people shall not be cut off from the city. Then the Lord will go forth and fight against those nations, as when he fights on a day of battle. On that day his feet shall stand on the Mount of Olives . . . you shall flee, as you fled from the earthquake in the days of Uzziah king of Judah. Then the Lord your God will come, and all the holy ones with him (Zech. 14 RSV).

And the prophet Malachi, in the passage which has enormously influenced the New Testament, says, 'Behold, I will send you Elijah the prophet before the great and terrible day when the Lord comes. And he shall turn the heart of the fathers to the children, and the heart of the children to their fathers, lest I come and smite the earth with a curse' (Malachi 4, 5–6). So the message of the New Testament is not without precedent in the Old, and it is instructive to ask what is it in the Old Testament and the New which creates this association between universal disaster and the coming of the Lord?

The Hebrews were, for the greater part of their history, a persecuted people, enjoying only relatively short periods of tranquillity and self-rule. In the main, they found themselves isolated in a world of superpowers, vulnerable to the nations on their borders and ultimately without any national home of their own. When Jerusalem was destroyed in 586 BC they lost, so it seemed, their only security on earth, and it is understandable that they should seek their security elsewhere. Their ultimate security, as the Pentateuch suggests and the prophets affirm, was that they believed in a God who reigned over all the nations and held them in the hollow of his hand.

The nations might rage, they might destroy, they might tyrannise, but in the end God himself, the God of the Hebrews, was in control. The day would come when the situation would be revealed for what it was – the nations crushed, God supreme, Israel secure. This is the message of the prophets. They were heavily involved in the moral issues of their day and in the political decisions of their nation. They had a good deal to say about war and peace, about riches and poverty, about treaties and covenants, about arms and about disarmament, but they had even more to say about the transcendent God who called out the stars by number and regarded the nations as a drop in the bucket, who created the world and presided over its destiny.

Like the Hebrews of the pre-Christian era and the Christians of the early Christian era, we live in a world which can never be secure. We live for ever now with the fear of nuclear disaster either as a consequence of military action or of industrial accident. The secret of nuclear power cannot be disinvented; the research laboratories of the world cannot be dismantled. There is no system of surveillance, however extensive and exact, which can actually prevent the manufacture of nuclear weapons. So while we have to do everything in our power to reduce the likelihood of nuclear disaster, we cannot again ever exclude it. From now on every generation will be aware that it could be the last generation on the earth. In a curious way, therefore, we find ourselves back in the mental climate of the New Testament, and are perhaps better equipped to understand the nature of the Christian hope which they espoused and which the Church ever since, generally, has neglected. That hope does not reside just in scattered sayings of our Lord, or in the exact delineation of the future as in the synoptic gospels. It resides in the fundamental nature of the world and of Him who presides over it. It is common alike to the Old Testament and the New that we worship the Creator of the world who will not suffer even the folly or malice of men to overthrow His purpose, who will provide for those who believe in Him a security which transcends all hopes and fears, and who will ultimately ensure that His will is done on earth as it is in heaven. I can hardly do better than quote from a lecture by the late Bishop of Bradford, given when he was Bishop of Hull.

> I imagine that every responsible person alive today lives in the awareness that we have, through the exercise of our God-given powers, developed the capacities either to exhaust the earth's resources or to destroy a large part of the cosmos and those who live in it. No Christian will reflect on these considerations other than with the most desperate seriousness. But my own instincts make me hesitate to speak too glibly of man's power to destroy God's universe, or to join those who conceive that it will be some rash or wicked act of *man* that will finally bring human history to an end. I believe that with all the power that God has given to man it remains *God's* world; God who does not give his glory to another, and that man's wrongdoing, ignorance or folly cannot ultimately bring to nothing what God created good.

> We have here no continuing city, we never dwell secure. A shift in the winds which produce our climate, the slightest deviation in the speed of the rotation of the planet, the melting of the ice-caps, or the uncontrolled use of fossil fuels could bring about the end of all human life on the earth. The world may not end with a bang; it could end with a whimper. Either way, the Christian hope provides, I believe, the only sure remedy for men and women who are afraid of what is happening on the earth. The hope of the coming of the Son of Man is not the product of a diseased imagination, it is of the essence of our faith in the God who created and sustains the universe. With our forefathers in the faith we ought perhaps to be saying, more in joyful expectation than in craven fear, the old Aramaic greeting which was part of the liturgy of the early Church – Maranatha, Lord come.

1 Tuchman, Barbara, *The Distant Mirror* (Macmillan, 1979).

For Discussion

1. What do you think it means to live by faith in a world threatened by the Bomb?

2. What do Christians hope for?

Section V
TWO POSTSCRIPTS

9 POLITICS AND THE ROAD TO PEACE
John Selwyn Gummer, MP

The road to peace is a continuous journey. People talk of it as if at some point there is an answer which can guarantee us immunity from war. Even in secular terms this is not a sensible concept; in Christian terms it seems totally contrary to the Gospel. There is no perfect position in which we can relax and say that peace has been achieved; no perfect position that is – outside the coming of the Kingdom of God.

Yet it is this thought that somehow we can reach a world without fear of war which gives the unilateralist argument attraction. It is certainly to this belief that young people clutch when they deploy CND's argument.

Now I know that this is not what the unilateralists claim, but it is how their claim is perceived, and it is that perception which very much affects the way in which the 'peace movement' is now moving. The heady days when unilateralism seemed poised to win the political battle in Europe have receded, and the movement has settled down to a comfortable reiteration of the old themes.

The key to this change has been the installation of Cruise and Pershing missiles; the 'peace movement' believed that the increase in international tension was the result of the West's intention to respond to the Russian build-up of SS20s and Backfire Bombers with this deployment. What was actually true, of course, was that the Soviet Union increased tension in order to prevent deployment. They felt that they had a very good chance of using the open societies of the West at their most vulnerable point. The very freedom which we seek to defend provides our opponents with the opportunity to make public opinion work against defence policies.

They, therefore, increased tension not *because* of the stationing of the Cruise missile but in order to prevent that stationing. They were very disappointed with election victories in Germany and Britain which defeated that manoeuvre. Yet the significance of the situation has still to be grasped by many supporters of CND. Indeed it appears to have escaped more moderate men in the Churches who seek to find a middle way. In February 1984, the Bishop of Birmingham introduced into the Synod a motion attributing increased tension to the deployment of Cruise and Pershing missiles. In fact, of course, since deployment the tension between East and West has declined. There is now no reason for it, for the Soviet Union has failed in its attempt to keep its superiority in missile deployment.

It may be thought surprising that a Christian's comments on the way in which the debate on the bomb will recede should start with so 'political' a perspective, but in fact, of course, it is absolutely crucial that Christians should be informed of the facts if they are to apply their moral judgments to decision-making. Once we move beyond the general condemnation of war and determination for peace, into the presentation of a practical programme for achieving it, then we owe it to the world to be most careful and rigorous in our assessment of the facts.

The weakness in the multilateralist case has always been that the slow pace of disarmament talks and the undramatic nature of negotiation in Vienna and Geneva has made it difficult for us to appear as concerned about peacemaking as we are about defence. The major change in this debate is, therefore, the way in which the deployment of Cruise and Pershing followed by the clear signals of Mrs Thatcher's visit to Hungary and President Reagan's *démarche* towards the Soviet Union have given a new impetus to the search for nuclear disarmament. The strategy is clear; by establishing the fact that the West is not prepared to allow weakness to encourage aggression it ensures that the Soviet Union has to come to terms with the world in which she will not achieve her ends by undermining the defence efforts of the free world.

This makes the conference table much more attractive a place and negotiations much more real. The economic problems which face Russia mean that they have a great interest in reducing a military build-up. The only argument against this is the belief that military build-up in the USSR will frighten the West's electorate into demanding unilateral nuclear disarmament.

The tentative movements which the new Russian leadership are beginning to make towards a resumption of talks will produce a more favourable atmosphere. The debate on unilateralism will increasingly be one in which CND in general, and Christian CND in particular, will have to come to terms with the fact that a real accord between East and West depends upon the certainty of the failure of unilateralism. If Russia ever again believes that there is a chance of the 'peace movements' succeeding then progress towards real disarmament will be severely interrupted.

For Christians nuclear weapons pose a great dilemma. It is obviously unacceptable to us that men should conceive of using such terrible destructive power, yet it is not the Christian way to throw our hands up in horror and say these things are too terrible for us even to be involved in. We have to admit that in a world which has invented nuclear weapons the Genesis story has a real application. We have eaten of the tree of knowledge and we cannot unlearn what we know.

Somehow we have to control that knowledge, and Christians will have to be in there pressing home the need to control the devastating forces which we now command. The coming debate is not about unilateralism or multilateralism, it is about how Christians can use their influence to press home the opportunities for peacemaking which the strength and determination of the West have made possible.

The argument will increasingly highlight a major difference in emphasis. The unilateralists are basically concerned with disarmament. They are committed to the proposition that the destruction of weapons is the key to peacemaking. Yet there is very little objective evidence which leads to this conclusion. Our concentration ought surely to be primarily on peace-keeping and only secondarily upon disarmament. We have managed to keep the peace in Europe since 1945; there have been neither nuclear nor conventional wars. Outside Europe in parts of the world where the deterrent is not operated, many millions have died unprotected by the nuclear umbrella.

If one starts, therefore, with peace-keeping it has to be accepted that NATO has been pretty successful in preventing war. The unilateralist does not start with peace-keeping but with arms reduction, and he is, therefore, prepared to put peace at risk in order to reduce arms. This is surely to make the method more important than the ultimate intention. The first challenge to the Christian is not whether the Bomb is an acceptable method of deterrence; instead it is 'how do we control the use of these weapons', or more bluntly 'how do we keep the peace'.

The moral problem then is simply whether the aggressor is more likely to use force where there is certainty of nuclear retaliation than where the victim has given up these weapons.

Nor is it just a case of seeing to it that *nuclear* war is prevented. It is also a matter of stopping conventional war in Europe. That is self-evident. If a conventional war were to start it would not matter what treaties, or what undertakings had been agreed, the risk is that at the point where defeat seemed inevitable the losing side would be bound to use nuclear weapons.

You cannot, therefore, opt out of the nuclear age by sticking to conventional weapons, that is why the Bishop of Birmingham's proposal to support a 'no first use of nuclear weapons' did not meet the Christian dilemma. If by giving up the use of nuclear weapons we were to encourage the Soviet Union to launch a conventional attack then there would be a high probability that in the face of such an attack, threatening the freedom of the historic powers, they would respond with nuclear arms. To pretend otherwise is to bilk the issue. If, however, we stick to the much more Christian statement that we forswear 'first use of force' then we meet the Christian demand. Once we have nuclear knowledge any conventional war in Europe must make nuclear war likely; our effort ought, therefore, to be to prevent any appeal to force. I am sure that had the Synod of the Church of England had time to debate the Bishop of Birmingham's 'no first use of nuclear weapons', and certainly had it had the right to amend his proposal, then the argument condemning no first use of force would have won the day.

We are now entering a new phase in the nuclear debate; it is becoming more clear that biological and chemical weapons can be as devastating as the nuclear bomb. We are beginning to understand that any war can lead to the use of nuclear weapons and that no hard and fast line can be drawn between modern methods of destruction. Even more important, we do now widely accept the principle that those who are strong enough to defend themselves are also strong enough to seek peace and to keep it. Those who run down their defences and open themselves to nuclear blackmail are not strong enough to seek peace nor secure enough to achieve it.

Instead of concentrating upon disarmament and selective weapons control, the Christian ought to get his priorities right. Our first job is to prevent war. The retention of our nuclear deterrent is an essential part of keeping the peace. To get rid of it would be to place disarmament before peacekeeping and that would be neither rational nor Christian.

THE CHURCH AND THE ROAD TO PEACE
The Rt Revd John Austin Baker

The public debate in which *The Church and the Bomb* played a not unworthy part has defined three areas in which there is urgent work for those Christians who are called by God to serve the cause of genuine and stable peace and disarmament.

Theology

The first area, as always, is that of theology. The Church of England is still far from having taken on board the theological material in *The Church and the Bomb*, but questions not treated there have also come to light.

One is the vision of biblical apocalyptic, and what relevance this may have for our attitude to the possibility of nuclear war. In discussion so far there has been a tendency to mix various biblical images without much regard to their original meaning and context. Thus, passages such as the so-called 'Little Apocalypse' in the first three Gospels (Mark 13; Matthew 24; Luke 21) are pressed into service, in particular because of the verse, 'When these things begin to come to pass, then look up, and lift up your heads; for your redemption draweth nigh' (Luke 21: 28 AV). But the end of the world in this prediction is a cosmic catastrophe brought about by direct divine action, including the overthrow of the spiritual powers of evil pictured as dwelling in the stars, not the result of human conflict. Similarly, the prophecy of the battle of Armageddon, derived by the author of Revelation from Ezekiel and other sources, has been used to show that the Bible envisages life on this planet ending as the result of a stupendous final conflict. But Armageddon is not a war between the forces of good and the forces of evil, but the mutual self-destruction of the wicked and godless nations, a battle in which the saints take no part. This may be a very plausible scenario for the final chapter of human history, but it hardly justifies Christians (as it is sometimes alleged to do) in the use of nuclear weapons as a means of defending righteousness. A much more subtle approach to this notoriously difficult type of material is required before it can be seen whether its essential message as revelation has anything to teach us in this particular perplexity.

Another question which is rightly urged is that of a coherent theology of power. Has Christian thought really engaged with the problems faced by those in government of every kind, and the right limits of the power allowed to them by God? All societies permit their rulers to do things not permitted to the ordinary citizen. If this were not so, civilised community life would be impossible, for reasons which stem partly from human sinfulness, partly from the inevitable clashes between objectives, good in themselves, which individuals make their own. This is in the nature of fallen creation, and the powers which bring order and approximate justice into this distorted world may be seen, and are seen in Scripture, as having a divine authority and a redemptive purpose. But how far are the methods they use to serve this purpose modified by God's revelation in Christ?

This leads directly into the question of Christian pacifism with which the Working Party felt itself unable to deal adequately. This issue has been endlessly debated without much progress on either side in converting the other. The advent of nuclear and other weapons of mass destruction, genetic damage and environmental pollution has, however, given the problem a new urgency in the minds of many Christians. It may well be that the terms of the question need to be broadened. For one thing, it clearly cannot be treated fairly without some agreement on what Jesus saw as the relation of his Church to the world. From there alone can we hope to develop a common mind on our Gospel calling as members both of the Church and of the human community at large.

One particular recent development in this connection, however, calls for immediate comment. It is basic to the nuclear arms dilemma that nations which feel themselves threatened by a nuclear-weapons power regard their own conventional forces, however strong, as in the last resort no effective defence. They can always be overcome by nuclear attack. Opposition to nuclear weapons, even when combined with support for conventional defence is therefore seen as essentially a form of pacifism, since it guarantees defeat in such a conflict, and so makes it futile to engage in it in the first place. In the pre-nuclear age pacifists could be 'carried' in the interests of other values, and as posing no serious threat to security. Today there is a growing intolerance in some quarters of pacifists and of the unilateralists who are bracketed with them. It is of the first importance that the Churches should resist this trend, and stand up for the rights of those who are called to live out the teaching of Jesus in their individual lives.

Public Policy

The public debate has also made it clear that, if the churches are to exercise any significant influence at all on policy, they have to be prepared to put their names to concrete and particular recommendations. General disapprobation of war is not enough. Like it or not, therefore, some Christians have got to understand the technical intricacies not just of armaments but of international politics, negotiations and so forth. No worth-while moral influence can be exerted without readiness to do this, and to engage in genuine and confidential dialogue with those who make decisions.

In this sphere there are encouraging developments in some of our universities and institutions of higher education, where staff are giving generously of their time and expertise to intellectual analysis of the whole range of problems connected with peace, and to positive proposals. The Churches should be openly supporting these efforts, and, where capable of doing so, sharing in them. In particular two subjects call for rigorous examination: one is the deterrence theory itself, and its manifest outworkings in strategy and the arms race; the other is the theory and practice of peace-building.

All the larger Churches in Britain have now made statements in this field which concern public policy. The time has surely come for some combined document, backed by the official approval of all the participating Churches, and so possessing real authority both within the Christian fellowship and in the nation. It would, no doubt, not be extreme in its recommendations; though it might, for example, take seriously the actual resolution of the February 1983 debate, which has fallen into oblivion. It ought to deal with some fundamental areas of possible misunderstanding, such as the concept of parity. It would need to be fairly short. But it could establish a line behind which the Churches were not prepared to fall. And it could refuse to be sucked into the oversimplifications of the unilateralist-multilateralist controversy, a mistake which *The Church and the Bomb* tried to avoid, but failed.

'Blessed are the peacemakers'

Such a document would, one might hope, cover more topics than just disarmament. Indeed, there could be a case for concentrating on some more general policy requirements, fulfilment of which is absolutely necessary if any progress is to be made in the matter of weapons.

The Church and the Bomb made quite a number of positive recommendations in this wider field which have virtually been ignored because of the controversy over UK weapons policy. It is more than time that these were actively explored. The Board for Social Responsibility, now that its anxieties over the UK's own nuclear weapons position have been allayed, might consider doing justice to some of these other points.

Two, in particular, offer real scope for Christian action. The first is that of the language of public statement and debate. The Archbishop of Canterbury drew attention in a memorable speech to the way in which cosy technical jargon can anaesthetise us against the human realities of nuclear war. Equally important is a campaign against the way in which the aggressive rhetoric of international affairs rubs us raw. If a nation has made what it considers to be adequate provision for its own security, then it has nothing to gain and much to lose by, for example, trading insults with other states, or instantly dismissing every proposal of the other side as worthless or fraudulent. Such verbal posturings may be an equivalent of gestures and display in the animal kingdom, designed to frighten off an enemy. Human affairs have new dimensions which render them sterile or dangerous.

Closely related to the language question is that of information. Various attempts are being made to disseminate accurate and balanced knowledge more widely as a background to public discussion of issues relating to peace. The Churches again could do much by being actively involved in this work.

The road to true peace in the world is long and hard. The Churches do not fulfil their duty by passing a resolution and then turning back to other things. We are going to have to commit a sacrificial proportion of prayer, toil and suffering to this cause for a long time to come.